Algrove Publishing Limited
36 Mill Street, P.O. Box 1238
Almonte, Ontario
Canada K0A 1A0

Telephone: (613) 256-0350
Fax: (613) 256-0360
Email: sales@algrove.com

Cover photo is of blacksmith Ronald Giroux in the shop at Upper Canada Village in Morrisburg, Ontario, Canada. Photo location courtesy of St. Lawrence Parks Commission.

Library and Archives Canada Cataloguing in Publication

Drew, James M. (James Meddick), b. 1863
    Farm blacksmithing / J.M. Drew.

(Classic reprint series)
Reprint. First published: St. Paul : Webb Pub. Co., 1901.
ISBN-10 1-894572-92-0
ISBN-13 978-1-894572-92-7

    1. Blacksmithing. I. Title. II. Series: Classic reprint series (Almonte, Ont.)

TT220.D74 2004   682   C2003-906503-0

Printed in Canada
#4-9-06

Publisher's Note

The great advantage of early books on crafts is that they were usually written by craftsmen who became instructors later in life, as opposed to many modern books written by observers of craftsmen.

The difference is important. This book is not a complete course in blacksmithing; it focuses on what you need to know to do very basic work. As in any activity, early success is necessary to build the confidence to try the more complex work that broadens and deepens skill levels.

J. M. Drew knew his craft as well as knowing where students of it usually encountered difficulty. He taught from a solid experience base.

Leonard G. Lee,
Publisher
November 2003
Almonte, Ontario

Warning

This is a reprint of a book published in 1901. It describes what was done and what was recommended to be done in accordance with the knowledge and practices of the day. It should be read in this light.

Two examples? On page 31 it's suggested that you sprinkle cyanide of potassium on hot iron to case-harden it. On page 59, you are encouraged to use red prussiate of potash (potassium ferricyanide) for the same purpose. Fortunately, current laws on the control of poisonous substances make both very difficult to obtain, but you should always question similar advice in all old books or reprints of old books.

We used to treat lead casually until we found that it accumulated in our systems. Treat all chemicals with respect and always use them only in ways sanctioned by the sellers and the law.

FARM BLACKSMITHING

BY

J. M. DREW.

Instructor in Blacksmithing, School of Agriculture,
University of Minnesota.

ST. ANTHONY PARK, MINN.

ST. PAUL
WEBB PUBLISHING COMPANY, PRINTERS
1901

INTRODUCTION.

A workshop on a farm is always a good sign. It is an indication that the farmer believes in having a place where he may profitably spend his time on stormy days that would otherwise be wasted. To such farmers, and their sons, this book is addressed, in the hope that they may learn from it some useful lessons in an easier way than by hard experience.

Several years ago a series of articles on "Farm Blacksmithing" appeared in Farm, Stock and Home. There was then, and has since been, some inquiry for a book embodying those articles and covering the subject of iron and steel work, or so much of it as the farm mechanic would need to know. Such a book has now been prepared, and the author has added to it such knowledge as he has gained by an experience of seven years in teaching blacksmithing to the farmer boys in the Minnesota School of Agriculture.

If the expert blacksmith complains that he finds nothing to interest him in the book, let him remember that it is not intended that he should. It was written for beginners.

The chapter on "Saw Filing" was written by Mr. William Boss, Instructor in Carpentry at the School of Agriculture.

FARM BLACKSMITHING.

The thoughtful reader will at once recognize the difficulty of teaching even the elements of a trade on paper; but I hope by the aid of illustrations to make reasonably plain all the operations which enter into the work which the farm blacksmith will be called upon to do.

Nowadays a farm blacksmith shop may be very cheaply furnished with all the tools necessary for ordinary work, and the convenience—yes, the necessity—of a forge on every farm needs no argument.

The time that may often be saved by having at hand the means and skill to repair damages to machinery and tools is often a much more important matter than the cash saved by doing one's own work. What farmer has not often been obliged, by some slight breakage, to go to the town or village shop,—perhaps several miles away,—and there find that he must wait for several horses to be shod before his little job, (which he might have done himself if he had the proper tools), could be attended to by the blacksmith.

While it is true that a man may work for a lifetime at a blacksmith's forge and still have more to learn about the trade, it is also true that the essentials of the trade consist of only a few comparatively simple operations, which may be acquired by any one who has mechanical ability and will give a little time and attention to the work. After this is done, skill will come with practice.

We are too apt to think that we cannot do a thing simply because we have never tried to do it, or anything like it.

"Our doubts are traitors; they make us lose the good we oft might win by fearing to attempt."

There is no good reason why every farmer who has any mechanical ability, cannot do nine-tenths of the work which he usually hires done by the blacksmith.

FURNISHING THE SHOP.

In furnishing a shop, the first thing to be considered is the forge. There are good portable forges now on the market which may be had for a reasonable price. To any one thinking of buying one of these I would say: Don't get one that is too small. One with a fire pan 18x24 inches and a 14-inch fan is small enough. The little bench forges are entirely too small for ordinary work.

A cheap forge which will answer every purpose of the ordinary farm shop may be made of wood,—simply a box filled with clay. It should be about three feet square and two and one-half feet high. A 36-inch bellows may be had for $5, and a single nest tuyere iron for 35 cents. A tuyere iron which may be cleaned out from the bottom will cost about $2. A very cheap and good tuyere may be made of a piece of two-inch iron pipe extending entirely through the forge. Several

small holes are drilled into the top side of the pipe for
the blast, and a plug is fitted into the end opposite the
bellows.   When the pipe gets clogged with ashes the
plug is pulled out, when a strong blast from the bellows
will blow everything out.   The picture on page 4
shows the style of forge in use at the School of
Agriculture.   It is simply a length of sewer pipe set on
end and filled with clay.   A hole is drilled through the
back side for the horn of the bellows, and an ordinary
single nest tuyere iron is used.   The bellows is an ordinary old-fashioned one, 32 inches wide.

The most expensive part of the outfit will be the anvil.   It has always been supposed that the best anvils
were those imported from England.   They cost about
10 cents per pound.   Very good American anvils can
now be had for about 8 cents per pound.   One weighing 80 to 100 pounds is none too large for a farmer's
use.   Don't make the mistake of getting a cast iron anvil that will not stand hard pounding.   The same is
true of the vise.   Get one that you can pound on without fear of breaking.   A wrought iron vise with steel
jaws costs from $3.50 to $5, according to weight.

A machinist's hammer, shown at Fig. 1, weighing

FIG 1.

one and one-half pounds, will be found the most conven-

ient size for common use, and a blacksmith's hand hammer weighing two and one-half pounds will be convenient to have at hand for heavier work.   Each will cost
about 50 cents.   For sharpening plows a round-faced
hammer should be used.   More will be said on this subject in a later chapter.   At the start the beginner will
need a pair of plain tongs (Fig. 2) and a pair of bolt
tongs (Fig. 3.)

FIG 2.

FIG. 3

The plain tongs may be changed into chain tongs by
cutting off the corners and shaping the ends of the jaws,
as explained on page 41.

This does not affect their usefulness as plain tongs,
and makes them serviceable in handling links and rings.

A set of stocks and dies for cutting threads on bolts
from one-fourth to three-fourths of an inch is almost a
necessity.   These will cost from $3 to $10, or even

more, depending upon kind, quality, and the number of sizes in the set. A good set for ordinary use, cutting three different numbers of thread, and taking bolts or nuts from five-sixteenths to three-fourths of an inch, may be had for $3. A very good upright drill press may be bought for $4.50.

The expense so far is about as follows:

Bellows and tuyere iron	$5.35
Anvil	8.00
Vise	4.00
Hammer	1.00
Tongs (two pairs)	.70
Hardy	.25
Stocks and dies	3.00
Drill press	4.50
Total	$26.80

Beside tools there will be needed a supply of blacksmith's coal and some iron and steel. For general blacksmithing, what is known as "Cumberland" coal is the best fuel. It contains but little sulphur, and is easily packed about the fire. It gives a powerful heat, and is so free from earthy matter that but little clinker is left after burning.

In former years charcoal was used almost entirely by blacksmiths. It has the advantage over other coals that it contains no sulphur, and for this reason is especially desirable for fine steel work. But its cost as compared with mineral coal has nearly driven it out of use. Ordinary stove coal, either hard or soft, cannot be used for blacksmithing. It contains such a large percentage of sulphur and other impurities that iron cannot be welded with it, and steel would be ruined if brought in contact with it while hot. Iron cannot be welded in the presence of sulphur. Great care should therefore be exercised to avoid getting sulphur into the forge. Never allow lead or babbit metal to be melted in the forge without a thorough cleaning out afterward. Iron and steel unite readily with sulphur to produce iron sulphide,—a brown powder which resembles neither iron nor sulphur. When sulphur is present iron at welding heat is slippery, whereas without the sulphur it would be sticky.

IRON AND STEEL.

It is necessary, or at least desirable, that the young blacksmith should know something about the nature of the materials he is to work with. He, of course, knows in a general way something about the different kinds of iron, (cast iron, wrought iron, malleable cast, etc.), which he sees all about him; and, has, as a rule, a general knowledge of steel and the uses to which it may be put. He has heard of cast steel, tool steel, machine steel, and Bessemer steel, and has perhaps a somewhat dim idea of what is meant by each of these terms.

Let us in a few words define the different kinds of iron and steel, and show how each is made and for what it may be used.

Iron, as every school boy knows, is mined in many parts of the world where it is found mixed with stone and other materials. This mixture is called "ore," and may be in the form of solid rock or a brown powder or dust. Iron is seldom found in the pure state, but there is a great difference in the purity of the ores found in different parts of the world. This fact will be referred to later.

The iron is separated from the ore by a melting process called "smelting," which consists in melting the ore by great heat so that the iron will flow out in a liquid form. This liquid is not pure iron, but contains more or less impurities, depending upon the purity of the ore from which it is smelted. From the smelter the liquid iron flows out in a trench in the earthen floor, and is led into little side trenches of the right size to make a lump of iron which may be handled by one man. These lumps are called "pig iron," from the fancied resemblance to a litter of pigs which a row of them presents when in the trenches. For a like reason the large trench is called the "sow."

Common cast iron is made by melting pig iron or a mixture of pig iron and old cast scrap iron and pouring it into molds. The proper mixing of the materials is of great importance in making good castings.

Malleable cast iron, or, as it is more commonly called "malleable iron," is common cast iron from which the carbon has been baked by long-continued heating in red-hot ovens. It is the usual practice to bake it for seven days. By baking out the carbon the iron is made much less brittle, and hence is useful for a great many more purposes than the common cast iron.

Wrought iron, as we usually see it, is made of old wrought iron scrap, which is worked over by being done up in bundles held together by wire or band iron, heated to welding heat and run between rollers to give it the required shape and size. In reworking old scrap great care must be taken to use only wrought iron scrap, and pickers are employed to carefully exclude all pieces of cast iron and steel; for if any of these materials get into the bundles the result will be too much carbon, which will cause the iron to be harsh and brittle, instead of malleable and tough.

The best wrought iron for purposes where great toughness is required comes from Sweden, but is commonly known to the trade as "Norway iron." It is very tough, because it is free from carbon and other impurities. The ore from which it is made is the finest iron ore known, and for this reason is used for making the finest grades of tool steel. No scrap iron is used in making Swedish iron.

STEEL.

Steel is simply iron to which has been added a very small amount of carbon. Carbon is one of the most common substances. We are most familiar with it in the form of charcoal. The diamond is almost pure carbon.

There are other elements to be found in steel in very small amounts, but for all practical purposes if we take pure iron and add to it a small percentage of carbon we will have steel. Steel such as is used for making cold chisels contains less than 1 per cent of carbon.

In the usual process of making fine tool steel, rods of pure wrought iron are packed in charcoal in long iron troughs, or boxes, which are sealed with fire clay and placed in a furnace, where they are subjected to a high heat for several days. The heat is so regulated that the rods do not melt, but are kept near the melting point. During this process the iron absorbs some of the carbon from the charcoal, and is thus changed to steel. The proper amount of carbon is determined by drawing out one of the rods occasionally and testing it. The steel made by this process is called "blister steel," for the reason that the surface of the rods is covered with small blisters. What is known as "shear steel" is made by heating these rods of blister steel and welding them together under a steam hammer, or by running them between rolls.

"Cast steel" is made by melting blister steel in earthen pots called "crucibles" and pouring into molds forming ingots, which are afterwards heated and rolled or hammered out into bars.

It will easily be seen that cast steel is much better for all tools than blister steel or shear steel, because the melting insures a thorough mixture of the carbon so that all parts are sure to contain the same amount. In blister steel the outside portions of the rods contain a much greater percentage of carbon than the centers; and in the shear steel the welding process does not cause such a complete mixture as in the process of melting which cast steel undergoes.

What is known as "mild steel," or "machine steel," is a steel which contains so little carbon that it is practically of the same nature as good wrought iron, excepting that it is somewhat stiffer and more durable when subjected to wear. It is produced by several different processes, the most important of which are the Bessemer and the open hearth processes.

In the Bessemer process the pig iron is melted in a large crucible or converter, and air is forced through the molten metal from the bottom. This causes the carbon to burn out and leave a mass of nearly pure iron. Then a quantity of iron having a known percent-age of carbon is added, thus giving any desired percent-age of carbon to the steel.

The open hearth process consists in melting pig iron in large furnaces built of fire brick and keeping it at a very high temperature, until the impurities are practi-cally all worked or burned out, leaving a liquid mass of nearly pure iron, which is then poured into molds form-ing ingots. These ingots are afterwards heated and rolled the same as wrought iron.

These processes have been so cheapened recently that soft steel is largely taking the place of wrought iron for many uses. It is now cheaper than the better grades of iron, and is taking the place of iron in almost all cases excepting where extreme softness, (for example, the making of rivets), is required. For this purpose nothing is better than Norway iron.

Iron is the most useful of all the metals: First, be-cause of its great strength; secondly, because it is so easily forged or changed in shape when hot, but be-comes rigid, and at the same time tough, on being al-lowed to cool. Wrought iron and all the milder forms of steel may be readily welded below a burning temper-ature. Steels containing a high percentage of carbon (in general all tool steels) may be welded if protected from the air by borax or other flux which will withstand a high heat.

PRACTICE WORK.

Assuming that the beginner has the tools mentioned on the preceding pages, or at least the most necessary ones, (forge, anvil, hammer, and tongs), let us start a fire. The first thing a blacksmith should try to learn is how to manage his fire so as to get the greatest heat just where he wants it, with the least waste of fuel.

Start a fire by using pine shavings, or any material which would make good kindling for a fire in a cook stove. After getting a good blaze started, pack a little coal around, *not upon,* the kindling, so that it will take fire slowly. Now begin to blow gently. After having had a fire in the forge there will always be coke which may be used instead of coal in starting the fire; but for the first time we are supposed to have only wood and blacksmith's coal. Remember that coal should never be placed *upon* the fire, but *around* it. After being near the fire for a short time it is changed to coke by having all its sulphur and other impurities burned out of it. By continually packing the coal about the fire and crowding it toward the center the blacksmith keeps a supply of coke burning in the middle of his fire, where he needs the most heat, and prevents the fire from spreading. It is often of advantage to wet the coal about the fire in order to pack it harder and thus keep the fire confined to the middle.

Your fire will now present the appearance of a

mound of coal with a center of burning coke, and more
or less of an opening in the middle through which the
blast is coming. Experience will soon show how much
blast should be given. The stronger the blast the greater the heat up to the limit where the coke in the middle
of the fire begins to be lifted out of place.

As a first lesson in blacksmithing, let us make a poker
with which to manage our fire. Take a piece of half
inch round iron about two feet long. Heat one end to
a white heat for a distance of about three inches, and
bend in the form of an eye (See Fig. 5.) Now heat
the other end and flatten about four inches and bend
as shown in the cut.

FIG5.

MAKING A DOOR HOOK.

Next, let us try to make an ordinary door hook.
Take a piece of ¾ round iron two or three feet long.
Put one end in the fire so that there will be burning
coke both above and below it. Give blast enough to
heat it quickly, but not enough to blow the coke out of
the middle of the fire. Get the end of the rod up to a
white heat and square about four inches of it, as shown
at *a,* Fig. 6. Draw it out so that the corners will come
out square and sharp. After heating again, draw out
the end, as shown at *b.* The shoulder between the
small part and the original iron is made by holding
against the edge of the anvil and striking so that the

edge of the anvil will cut into the iron to form the shoulder. In drawing out iron to make a point on it or to make it smaller, always draw it square first, no matter what is to be its shape finally, for you can reduce its size faster by squaring it than by trying to keep it round or any other shape. Next make this small end round by flattening down the corners. Stop pounding and heat the iron as often as it gets below a cherry red in color. After rounding the end, turn it around the horn of the anvil to make a round eye. Next cut off the iron and draw out to a point, as at *e.* Complete the hook by bending the end and twisting the middle, as shown at *f.*

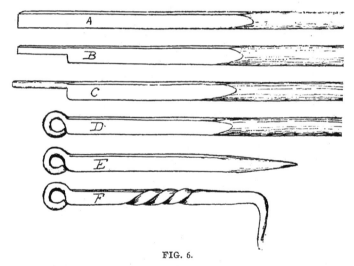

FIG. 6.

The beginner is apt to have trouble in getting the eye of the hook perfectly round. It usually persists in being oval, rather than circular. The trouble is usually caused by not bending the end enough at the start. The end must be given its full amount of bend before the other part is bent, as afterward it cannot be gotten at.

MAKING A STAPLE.

To make a staple draw out one end of a rod and round it, or leave it square, depending upon the kind of staple you want. Decide how long you want the staple, and bend the end at right angles to the remainder of the rod (Fig. 7), to form one leg of the staple. Do not make the complete bend at this time, or the finished end will be in the way when you sharpen the other end. Cut off the iron for the second leg a little shorter than the first, to allow for lengthening in drawing out to a point. Now draw out the second leg to a point, then heat in the middle and complete the bend.

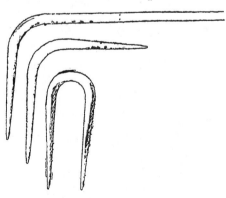

FIG. 7.

MAKING CHAIN.

Machine made chains are so cheap that no farm blacksmith can afford to make his own, but he will often be called upon to mend chains and supply missing or broken hooks and rings. To make a link, take a piece of $\frac{3}{8}$ inch rod, heat about three inches from the end, and bend so as to form the letter "U" (Fig. 8). Now cut off on the hardy, so that both legs of the U shall be of the same length (about three inches). Then holding the bent part with a pair of chain tongs, heat the two ends and scarf, (flatten), the inside corner of the left one. Now turn over and scarf the corresponding corner of the other leg. In doing this scarfing, do not flatten the whole end, as this would make the end of the link too thin. Simply flatten the inside corners a little. Next, bend the two legs so that the flattened or scarfed places shall come together and the ends cross each other at right angles. You are now ready to make your first weld. When iron is at welding heat it is perfectly white and the surface is in a melted condition. It presents the appearance of wet ice or snow,—exactly like a hard snowball that a boy has held for some time in his warm hands. To get the end of the link to the required heat, hold it in the center of the fire, (there should be burning coke both above and below it), and turn it over every few seconds to make sure of heating both sides alike. If it were held still in the fire the bottom side would burn before the top got hot enough to weld. When you have it at the right heat place it quickly upon the anvil and strike

first on one side and then on the other. Do not
strike a single blow after the iron gets below a welding heat, as that would only make the iron thinner
without doing the weld any good. Finish off the weld
over the horn of the anvil. Try to make the welded part
round and the same size as the balance of the link.
Your link will now be too wide at one end. To shape
it properly hold as at *d* in Fig. 8, and strike in the
place shown by the arrow. Beginners often make the
mistake of holding the link flat on its side when trying to shape it. The result is always something like
the shape shown at *f*. The correct shape is shown at *e*.
After a little practice one should be able to make a link
with only two, or at most, three heats.

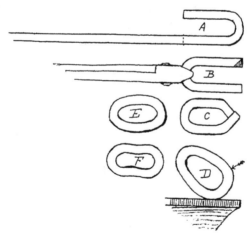

FIG. 8.

The greatest difficulty with most beginners consists
in getting the iron to a welding heat without burning.

The great majority try to weld before the iron is hot enough. The only safe way is to watch carefully and take the iron from the fire the moment the surface begins to flow and look wet. If you wait until the sparks begin to fly, the iron will be burning. With large irons no harm will be done if a few sparks are seen; but with small irons, and especially with mild steel, this is just beyond the danger line.

MAKING A RING.

To make a ring take a piece of $\frac{1}{2}$ or 7-16 in. iron a foot long, and upset both ends, as shown at a, Fig. 9.

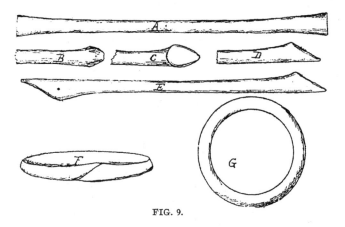

FIG. 9.

This upsetting is done by heating one end and holding it on the anvil and striking the other end. In doing this take a short heat, that is, heat only an inch or so of the end, and be careful not to let it get bent in upsetting. If it bends, straighten it at once. After upsetting both ends, heat one end and scarf it for welding. Do this by first holding it on the anvil at an angle of about 30 degrees, and striking with the hammer held at a corresponding angle. Strike a few blows, or until the iron assumes the shape shown at *b*. Now turn the iron a quarter turn, and lay it flat on the anvil and shape like *c*. *D* is another view of the same. In doing this do not strike straight down, but drive the iron back toward you. Next, treat the other end in the same way, being careful to make the scarf on the side opposite the first one, so that when the ring is bent the two scarfs will come together. Be sure to bend the ring as shown in the cut, so that in welding you can get at both ends of the scarfs with the hammer. After welding, work the iron around the weld down to its original size. Do not attempt to make a ring without first upsetting the ends, or you will find after welding that the iron is too small each side of the weld;—a condition which cannot be remedied. In making a ring for a chain, do not attempt to join to the chain before welding, but first finish the ring, then join to the chain by another link.

In case of a rush job, where appearances do not count for much, or where it will make no particular difference if there is a thin place in the ring, one may make a ring after the fashion of a chain link, rounding it up afterwards.

MAKING A CHAIN HOOK.

Two ways are here shown of making a chain hook.
The first is a good way when good iron is used.   The
iron is first upset, then rounded off.   Then a hole is
punched and worked out large over the horn of the
anvil, and the iron around the hole is rounded up at
the same time.   Next it is cut off and the end drawn
down to a blunt point and rounded.   It is next bent a
little over half way; then the back is beveled so that it is
quite thin; but the inside of the hook is left as thick as
possible.   The shaded portions in the figure marked *c*
show how it should look in cross-sections if cut through.

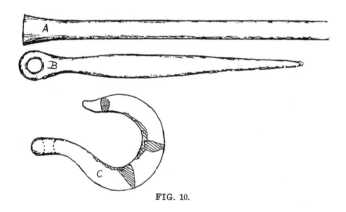

FIG. 10.

This exercise introduces an operation which we have
not met with before; that is, punching.

To punch a hole in iron, heat to white heat; hold on
the anvil, not over the hole, but over the solid face of
the anvil and drive the punch till it feels as though
it were solid against the face of the anvil; then turn
the iron over and you can see a clear round space
where the punch tried to come through. Place the
punch on this spot and drive it in; now place the iron
over the hole in the anvil and drive the punch through.
This will make a clean-cut, smooth hole, whereas if
it had been punched from one side only, a ragged hole
would have been the result.

Another way of making a chain hook is shown in
Fig. 11. This way is always to be preferred to the
one just described if the iron used is not very tough.

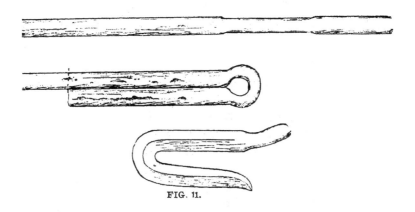

FIG. 11.

Smaller iron may also be used than in the first way,
because it is doubled where the most strength is re-

quired. The cut shows the method of making so clearly that little description is necessary.

The iron is usually drawn down a little in size where the eye is to be; then is bent and welded; then cut off and sharpened and bent the same as in the case of the first hook.

The beginner is quite apt to burn the iron around the eye before getting it hot enough where the weld is to be. It is a good plan to heat to near the welding point; then dip the eye part in water until it turns black; then reheat very quickly, and the eye part will not get too hot again before the other part is ready to weld.

A grab hook is made in the same way, only it is left square after welding, and then bent on the corner, as shown in Fig. 11. To start the bend right, place in the square hardy-hole in the anvil.

MAKING A CLEVIS.

There are several good ways of making a clevis. When good iron is used—that is, Norway iron, or any tough iron— about the best way is to upset and punch the ends the same as in beginning the first chain hook. A piece of ⅝ iron 13 inches long makes a good clevis. Upset both ends and the middle as shown in b, Fig. 12; then flatten out and punch the ends; then bend into shape. The holes should be large enough to take a half inch pin.

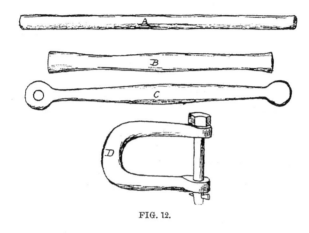

FIG. 12.

Another way to make a clevis, and the best way in case ordinary or poor iron is used, is to draw out the end square for about three or four inches, as shown in Fig. 13, and bevel off the end; then bend and forge a sharp angle, as shown at *a*, about two inches back towards you forge another angle (b). These angles are formed by bending the iron at nearly right engles, then hammering, as shown in the cut. It is not an easy thing to do, and requires practice to make a good job. After forming the angles, or corners, bend the iron so that the two corners will come together, forming a round eye. Now weld the end fast to the side and one end of the clevis is done. The other end is, of course, formed in the same way.

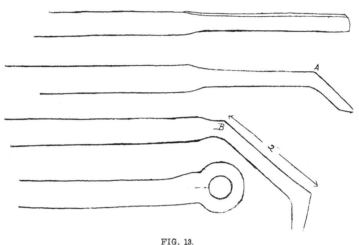

FIG. 13.

Another and quicker way of upsetting the end
(the way which is usually taken to make the end
of a brace) is shown at Fig. 14.   The end is bent at
right angles and flattened down, making a round lump.
The edges must be heated to welding heat and welded
down, or a crack will show where the flattened part
joins the other iron.

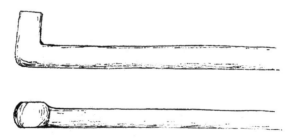

FIG. 14.

To make a clevis in the shortest possible time take
20 inches of 7·16 iron, bend in the middle to form a
long "U"; weld the ends together the same as in making a chain link. Now close the sides together, as in
Fig. 15, and bend to form a clevis.

FIG. 15.

After making a clevis we will want a pin or bolt
for it. This brings us naturally to the making of
bolts.

BOLTS.

It is much cheaper to buy bolts than to make them;
and if one could always have access to a stock of bolts
of all sizes and lengths, he need never take the time
to make one. But the farmer will often find himself
in need of a bolt which he has not in his assortment,
and if he can make one himself he is master of the
situation. Having a bolt of the right size, but too
long, it is an easy matter to cut it down to the required length and cut new threads.

The simplest way to make a head on a bolt is to up-

set the end until it is about a half larger in diameter
than the bolt; then drive into a heading tool (see Fig.
16). This is the way usually followed in making
small bolts. Large bolt heads are usually welded on. To
make a welded head, take round iron a size smaller

FIG. 16.

than the iron of the bolt. For example, if the bolt is
half inch iron, use 7-16 iron for the head. Form a
ring, or eye, in the end of the smaller iron by bending
around the horn of the anvil. This eye must be of a
size to loosely fit the bolt, and must be cut so as to
reach only about three-quarters of the way around (See
Fig 17).

FIG. 17.

After forming this eye, do not cut it entirely off
from the rod, but cut it nearly off; then heat the end

of the bolt and upset it a little in the eye, or ring; then break the ring loose from the rod, where it was nearly cut through, and hammer it so to make it clasp the end of the bolt tightly. Next heat to welding heat and weld. Don't be afraid to hit it hard. You will now see that the ring reaches entirely around the bolt. Had it been cut long enough at first to reach around it would have been apt to double up and cause trouble in welding.

After welding the ring to the end of the bolt, heat again to welding heat and drive into the heading iron, being careful to drive it straight down so as not to make a one-sided head. After flattening it down take it out and shape the head round or square, or hexagon, to suit your needs or fancy.

When a head is needed on a long rod, for instance a bridge rod, it is first formed on a short piece of rod, which is afterwards welded to the long rod.

HEADING TOOLS.

To make a heading iron upset one end of a piece of good iron (Norway is to be preferred), as shown in Fig. 16; then punch the hole the desired size, and either weld a piece of thin steel on the face side or case harden the face. In punching the hole, make it a taper hole, smallest at the face side. The face may be case hardened by heating to a good light red heat and sprinkling with powdered cyanide of potassium.

This chemical is a very strong poison, and should be kept in a safe place, away from the reach of children. The handiest way of applying it is to use an ordinary tin pepper box with perforated top.

A clevis bolt should have an eye, or slot for a key at the lower end. To make the slot, use a flat punch and after punching dress the bolt down to the proper size while the punch is still in place.

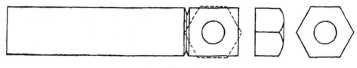

FIG. 18.

Fig. 18 shows how nuts may be made. Little explanation is necessary. The iron is drawn out the right width and thickness; then nearly cut off on the hardy; then the hole is punched. The sides are squared up while the punch is in the hole. In heating a nut after cutting it off from the bar, instead of handling it with a pair of tongs use a piece of wire, or a one-fourth inch rod with a short bend in the end.

As a general thing enough odd nuts may be found in the farmer's workshop, in which new threads may be cut, so that it will seldom be necessary to make new ones. The farm blacksmith will appreciate the need of saving all the old nuts and bolts to use in cases where they may save the necessity of making new ones.

Cutting threads on bolts is a very simple operation, and needs little description. The standard numbers of threads for carriage bolts are as follows:

1-4   in. bolts 20 threads to an inch.
5-16 "   "   18   "   " " "
3-8 "   "   16   "   " " "
7-16 "   "   14   "   " " "
1-2 "   "   12   "   " " "
5-8 "   "   11   "   " " "
3-4 "   "   10   "   " " "
1-   "   "   8   "   " " "

A set of stocks and dies to cut all of the above threads will cost about $12; but a set which will answer all ordinary purposes of the farm blacksmith need not cost more than three or four dollars. For this price one can get a set of taper taps and a stock containing three sets of dies, cutting 20, 16 and 10 threads to an inch, and which may be used on all sizes of bolts and nuts, from one-fourth of an inch up to three-fourths of an inch. In using either dies or taps, plenty of oil should be used; lard oil is best. Never use dies on steel or hot iron.

In using the ordinary stocks and dies to cut threads on a bolt, it is best to start at the bottom of the intended thread rather than to try to screw the dies on from the end of the bolt. It is much easier to get the dies started straight in this way.

In using taper taps for threading nuts the taps should be run in the same depth from both sides of the nut. When fitting a nut to a bolt, thread the bolt first then run the tap into the nut till the threads will fit the end of the bolt, then reverse the nut and run the tap in to the same depth from the other side.

The farmer's workshop should be supplied with an assortment of bolts, washers, screws, rivets, etc., which, if kept in order where a bolt or screw or rivet of any particular size and length may be found when wanted, will prove a great saving of time.

Much may be saved by buying such things in wholesale lots, rather than a few at a time: For instance, it is cheaper to buy a package of 50 carriage bolts than to pay the retail price for half that number.

A fairly complete list of carriage bolts would be made up of one package each of the following sizes and lengths:

$\frac{1}{4}$ diameter.		5-16 diameter	
Length.	Pr. Pkg. of 100.	Length.	Pr. Pkge of 50
$1\frac{1}{4}$	25c	$1\frac{1}{2}$	16c
$1\frac{1}{2}$	26c	2	17c
2	28c	$2\frac{1}{2}$	18c
$2\frac{1}{2}$	30c	3	19c
3	32c	$3\frac{1}{2}$	21c
$3\frac{1}{2}$	34c	4	22c
4	36c	$4\frac{1}{2}$	24c
$4\frac{1}{2}$	39c	5	25c
5	40c	$5\frac{1}{2}$	26c
$5\frac{1}{2}$	43c	6	28c
6	45c		

⅜ diameter		½ diameter	
Length.	Pr. Pkg. of 50	Length.	Pr. Pkg. of 50
1¼	................18c	2	................37c
1½	................19c	2½	................38c
2	................19c	3	................39c
2½	................21c	3½	................42c
3	................24c	4	................45c
3½	................26c	4½	................47c
4	................26c	5	................50c
4½	................29c	5½	................52c
5	................31c	6	................55c
6	................34c		

An assortment of washers for the different sizes of bolts should be kept.

WELDING.

Let us now try our hand at welding two irons together. So far, all our welding has been done with irons that would naturally stay together. Welding separate irons will be found to be quite a different matter.

Take two pieces of one-half inch iron; upset and scarf one end of each in exactly the same manner as in the case of the ring already described. Now see that you have a clean fire; that is, a fire with no clinkers or old burned out ashes at the bottom. Have a good bed of coke burning nicely and a supply of coal closely banked about it. Do not allow any fresh coal to come in contact with your irons. Put the irons in the fire face side down; that is, the scarf side down. Have burning coke both above and below the irons. Have your hammer lying at the right-hand end of the anvil, with the face side away from you, and be sure that you know exactly where it is, so that you can pick it up without having to look for it. To get the irons on the anvil in the right position without loss of time, take hold of the right hand one so that the back of your hand will be upward and the little finger toward the fire. This will naturally bring the scarfed side up when placed on the anvil. See Fig. 19. Practice this a

FIG. 19.

few times before heating the irons. By steadying the left hand iron on the edge of the anvil (Fig. 19), you can bring it down upon the other one in just the right position without any uncertainty. Irons at welding heat are very sticky, and if they happen to touch each other when in a wrong position will cause trouble.

Now heat to welding heat. Do not let one iron heat faster than the other. If one is inclined to do this, pull it back a little. When you get a nice welding heat on both irons take them out quickly (remembering to take hold with the right hand so as to bring the iron face side up on the anvil); strike them a sharp blow on the edge of the anvil, to shake off any dirt or scale that may be on them; then place the right-hand iron as in Fig. 19, and bring the other down upon it by guiding it from the edge of the anvil. If they are at the proper heat they will now stick together so that you can let go with the right hand and pick up the hammer. Strike a light blow first, then a heavy one, at the place indicated by the arrow in Fig. 20.

FIG. 20.

Turn the iron over quickly and strike in the same way on the other side. If the iron has cooled below the welding heat, put it back in the fire and heat again until the surface is in a melted condition; then go all around the weld, pounding it down to the original size of the iron. With large irons it is generally possible to make a perfect weld with one heat; but small irons lose their heat so quickly that it is generally necessary to heat two or three times before finishing.

After practicing with half-inch irons until you can make a good weld, try a smaller size. Also try welding a short piece to a long one by using bolt tongs for holding the shorter piece. Finally weld two short pieces, using two pairs of tongs. Where one pair of tongs is used, take the tongs in the right hand, and, after placing the left-hand iron on the right one, let the tongs drop to the floor while picking up the hammer.

Flat iron is welded in the same way as round, but is somewhat harder to make a good job with, as it is not easy to get all the corners and edges welded down so they will not show.

To weld flat iron at a right angle, upset slightly and draw out the side of each piece as shown in Fig. 21, and place together as shown. Never try to make a sharp inside corner in a weld of this kind, for if you do, a crack is almost sure to start there. Leave the inside rounding unless a square corner is absolutely required, in which case, file it square rather than try to forge it.

To weld flat irons in the form of a T, upset and scarf both the end, Fig. 22, and the place where it is to be welded on. Great care must be taken to have no scale or cinder in the hollow scarf at the time of welding.

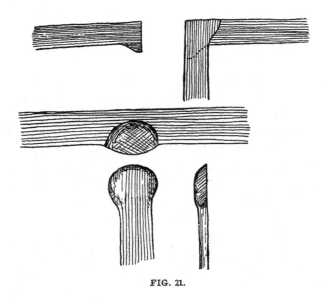

FIG. 21.

MAKING TONGS.

To make a pair of ordinary blacksmith's tongs take
a piece of three-fourths inch round Norway iron or
soft steel, heat one end, and placing it upon the anvil,
as at *a,* in Fig. 23, strike so as to drive it down past
the corner of the anvil to form a shoulder, next placing
it across the anvil at an angle of 45 degrees with
the length of the anvil, as at *c,* so that the inside angle
of the shoulder first formed comes just over the further

edge of the anvil, flatten down the part on the anvil about two inches back. This will make a beveled shoulder, as shown at c. E is another view of the same. Cut off at the dotted line in e. Draw out and round the end just cut off, and scarf it for welding on handle, as shown at g. Be sure to make the scarf on the same side as the beveled shoulder. Now lay this jaw aside and make another exactly like it; then take a piece of seven-sixteenths round iron or mild steel two feet long; upset both ends to the size of the scarfed ends of the jaws; scarf and weld a jaw to each end. Next cut in the middle and draw out and finish the ends; then punch the rivet holes, which should be about five-sixteenths of an inch in size. To make the rivet, draw out a piece of half-inch iron, as shown at h, leaving, a shoulder for the head of the rivet; cut nearly off on the hardy, so nearly that it can be easily broken off after being inserted in the jaws. Heat it white hot, insert, break off and rivet down. In riveting, do not strike a flat blow, but hold the hammer at an angle so as to give a beveled edge to the rivet head. If the riveting has tightened the jaws so that they do not work easily, simply heat red hot and open and shut them a few times while hot. If intended for chain tongs, cut off the corners as at l, and shape the ends of the jaws, as shown at m, by heating and bending over a piece of three-eighths inch iron or the end of a small punch.

To make a pair of bolt tongs draw out the iron as at Fig. 24; drawing it square first, then rounding. Shape the end by flattening out; then make the groove

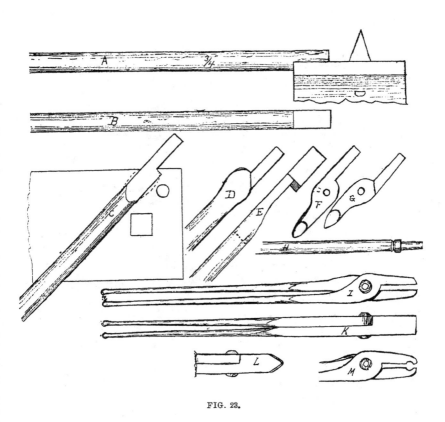

FIG. 23.

by placing the iron in the angle between face and horn
of anvil, and striking with the ball end of the hammer.
See Fig. 24 D. After bending the jaws, shape over
the shoulder of the anvil the same as in the case of the
plain tongs; then cut off and scarf for welding on the

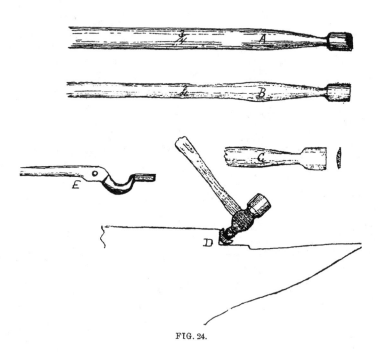

FIG. 24.

handle. After riveting the two jaws together the
grooves may be finished by heating hot and shaping
over a piece of round iron or the end of a punch.

Tongs of many shapes and sizes are useful for different kinds of work; but the two kinds just described
are used most often, and any one who can make them

can make any kind which his work may call for. Fig. 25 shows two kinds which will be found handy in many

FIG. 25.

ways. The first ones are used in dressing hand hammers and all anvil tools having eyes for handles. The second pair is used in dressing ball pein hammers or in handling short bolts. Horse shoer's tongs are usually made with short and wide jaws, usually rounded. See Fig. 26.

FIG. 26.

WHIFFLETREE IRONS.

Fig. 27 illustrates a good way of ironing singletrees. The end irons and hooks are made of 7-16 round iron and the middle iron is of 1-2 inch round. Fig. 28 shows the manner of making the hooks. It should be noticed that the end of the hook comes within 7-16 of an inch of touching the inside of the back of the eye. This prevents the tug from coming unhooked of itself. The hook has to be turned up as shown in the cut, (Fig. 27), before the tug can be hooked or unhooked.

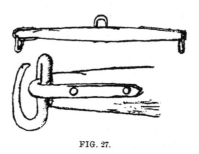

FIG. 27.

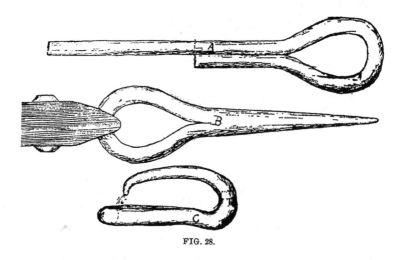

FIG. 28.

At Fig. 29 is shown the way to make a hook with a
bar across the end to prevent unhooking. The bar is
made by leaving a lump on the end when the hook is

drawn out and then flattening the lump in the vise and
drawing the ends out round over the edge of the anvil.

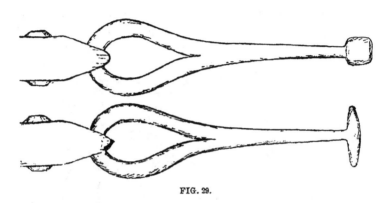

FIG. 29.

Another good, strong singletree is shown in Fig. 30.
It is made of hickory or oak 1¼ inches thick and two
inches wide, tapering to 1½ inches wide at the ends.
A strap of iron 3-16 inch thick and 1 inch wide runs
the whole length of the back and is fastened by screws.
The ends are turned over to make eyes for holding the
hooks.   The hooks have bars across the ends as shown
in Fig. 29.

FIG. 30.

MAKING A SWIVEL.

To make a swivel for an ordinary log chain, take a piece of Norway iron or mild steel about half inch by inch in size and draw out one end to about ⅜ inch and 3 inches long. Leave about one inch in length the original

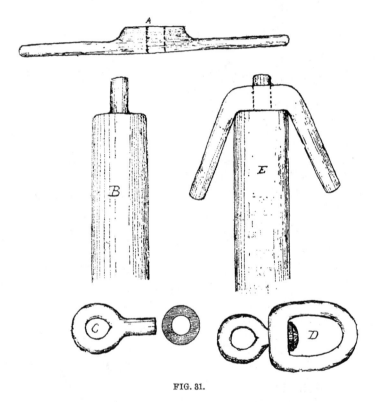

FIG. 31.

size of the iron and draw out another three inches to ⅜. See A in Fig. 31. Punch a half-inch hole in the

middle of the flat part. Next make a mandrel as
shown at B, of ⅜ inch round iron by drawing out a
short bit of the end to about 7-16 inch in size. Heat
the iron first made and work it into shape over the end
of the mandrel as shown at E. Next make the eye, C,
by bending and welding a piece of 7-16 inch iron, heat
it and insert the shank in the hole in A and put on a
washer and rivet down. Finish by welding the ends
of A the same as a chain link. D shows the completed
swivel.

FORGING AND TEMPERING STEEL TOOLS.

The making and tempering of simple steel tools,
such as cold chisels, drills, etc., and the welding and
sharpening of plow points, should be well understood
by the farm blacksmith.

Let us imagine that we have a bar of tool steel in
the fire and are about to make a very simple tool,—
say a cold chisel. The first and principal thing to have
in mind is that we must not *overheat* the steel. Steel,
owing to the carbon which it contains, is much more
easily burned than iron, and the beginner is almost
sure to burn the first steel he attempts to work, unless
he is warned in regard to it.

The fire for steel work should be clean; that is, it
should consist of a body of burning coke. Fresh coal,

owing to the sulphur which it contains, has a bad effect
upon steel. The steel must be heated slowly and even-
ly, in order to be of the same temperature and conse-
quently the same degree of softness throughout. If it
is heated too quickly the outside will be softer than the
center, and will be drawn out faster as we draw out the
end of the chisel, and though we cannot see any defect
at the time, a crack will be apt to develop when the
tool is tempered.

Heat to a light red or yellow color, and draw out to
the shape of a wedge. Hammer it on all sides alike
as nearly as possible. Do not let the sides spread out
like a dove's tail, but keep them straight with the
original bar.

Draw out somewhat thinner and longer than needed;
then cut off three-eighths or one-half inch, to insure an
edge of sound steel. Shape the head end as shown in
Fig. 32. Finish the forging by giving it a good hammering. By "good hammering" I mean a hammering
that shall refine the steel at the edge of the tool and
correct any overheating that it may have suffered while
being forged. By "overheating" is meant any heating
above the heat that will give the finest grain to the
steel when it is tempered. Overheating differs from
burning. Burnt steel cannot be refined or "restored."
Throw it away. Overheated steel may be refined or
restored to a fine grain by proper hammering while it
is at just the right heat. To do this to our chisel we
will heat it to a very dull red and hammer it quickly
on both flat sides (not on the edges), beginning with
quite heavy blows and striking lighter as the steel

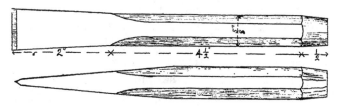

FIG. 32.

cools; stopping altogether as the red color disappears. This hammering will probably spread the edge of the chisel wider than you want it, but do not strike it on the edge, as that will undo what you have accomplished by hammering it on the sides. The sides can be ground off or filed off afterwards.

Before trying to temper the chisel we will allow it to cool slowly and then file it to an edge. While it is cooling, try the following experiment, which will show you, more plainly than any amount of reading, the effect of heat upon steel.

Take a bar of tool steel, and after heating it to a red heat notch it on the hardy so that it will be cut nearly half off every half inch of its length for three inches. Now hold and turn it in the fire in such a way that the extreme end will begin to burn and throw off sparks before the last section or notch becomes red. This will require considerable care in handling and turning the piece in the fire. The different sections should now form a gradual scale of color, from white and sparkling (burning), down through the different shades of a red to black. When it is in this condition take it from the fire and plunge it quickly into cold water and move it about so as to cool it as quickly as possible. When it is cold break each section off by holding the notch over the corner of the anvil and striking a blow with the hammer. The first two or three pieces will break off very easily, each succeeding section showing more toughness till the last, which will probably be very hard to break from the bar. After gathering up the pieces fit them together in their original positions; then turn the upper or bar end of each section towards you, and you will have an object lesson on the effect of different degrees of heat upon steel. The sections which were overheated show a coarse, hard grain, and, as we discover in breaking them, are brittle. This coarseness of grain diminishes as we go up the scale toward the place where the bar was heated to a dull red. Here we find the grain the finest; even finer than in the original bar. In the photo engraving the first two cuts show the grain of steel that has been overheated, No. 1 being much more badly burned than No. 2. No. 3, which was heated to a dull red, is seen to have the finest grain. No. 4 is the end of the original bar. It is thus seen that proper heating produces a finer grain than the original steel contained.

TEMPERING TOOLS.

The tempering of steel tools consists of two processes: First, hardening by heating, then suddenly chilling; and, second, "drawing the temper" or softening from the chilled state to the degree of hardness desired. In the case of the chisel which we were considering, we need to have only one end—the edge—hardened. To accomplish this, heat the whole chisel to a dark or cherry red color, and holding it perpendicularly over the water, dip the end in an inch or more and keep it moving up and down for a few seconds, or until the edge is cool enough so that the water will not dry on it for the space of two seconds when it is drawn out. Now polish one side quickly with a piece of brick so that the colors denoting the degree of heat may be seen. These colors will form a band which will be seen to move towards the edge or cooler part of the tool. First will be seen a pale yellow or straw color; then darker yellow, which changes to brown; then purple, then blue.

A cold chisel needs to be quite soft, so we will wait until the blue gets to the edge; then quickly dip the edge into the water again and hold it there until the remainder of the tool is cool enough so that we may dip the whole without fear of hardening it. Tools for woodwork, such as carpenter's chisels and plane irons, are tempered to a straw color, as they require a very hard edge in order to be kept sharp, and all boys know that they are not a success when used, as a cold chisel is, for cutting nails, etc.

Small articles, as penknife blades and all tools which require an equal temper throughout, are first chilled by being thrown into water when hot; then are heated to the required color by being held in a gas flame or laid on a bar of hot iron, and are dropped into the water again when the right color appears. In chilling the end of a chisel, drill, or any similar tool, it should not be held still in the water, as this is apt to start a crack at the water line. Dancing the tool up and down while chilling will lessen the danger of cracking. In retempering a tool it is a good plan to hammer it lightly before chilling, as this seems to lessen the liability of cracking.

Almost every cross-roads blacksmith has some particular receipt for a tempering fluid which he considers better than anything else for tempering tools. Plain water is as good as anything else for ordinary use. Salt water is often used in case it is necessary to make a tool very hard. Salt water will harden steel harder than pure water, simply because it is a better conductor of heat; but very few tools need to be made harder than water will make them. Oil is better than water in cases where it is desirable not to chill the steel too suddenly, as, for instance, in the case of thin knives or any tools which are liable to warp out of shape in cooling. A layer of oil on top of the water answers as well as all oil. Steel cannot be hardened in soapy water, for the reason that the soap in the water forms a coating on the steel the instant it comes in contact with it. This coating of soap is a poor conductor of heat, and prevents the steel from cooling suddenly.

The following table shows approximately the temperature (Fahrenheit) indicated by the colors on steel:

1. Very pale straw color...............430 deg.
      (Stone drills for hardest stone).
2. Yellow 450   "
      (Wood working tools, stone drills.)
3. Dark Yellow 470   "
4. Brownish yellow 490   "
      (Hammers.)
5. Brown 500   "
      (Lathe tools.)
6. Brown tinged with purple............520   "
      (Drills, hard.)
7. Light purple 525   "
      (Drills.)
8. Dark purple tinged with blue.........550   "
      (Watch springs, swords, hard cold chis
          els.)
9. Dark blue 565   "
      (Saws, cold chisels for soft iron.)
10. Very dark blue 500   "
      Saws, screw drivers.)
11. Dark blue tinged with green..........660   "
      (Too soft for any tools.)

No great amount of dependence should be placed
upon the above table as an absolute guide for practical
work, for the reason that steel varies in the degree of
hardness indicated by the colors for every variation
of carbon content. The greater the percentage of
carbon in the steel the harder will it be for each color.
For example: A cold chisel made of a certain brand
of steel may be just right for a certain kind of work
if tempered dark purple, whereas a chisel made from
a steel containing a higher percentage of carbon, in
order to stand the same work without breaking would
have to be let down to a blue color. The only way to
be sure of the proper tempering of a tool is to try it.
A toolsmith should never warrant tools made from a
new brand of steel until he has made and tried one
from that brand. A person may tell something about
the amount of carbon in an old chisel or stone drill by
the way the head turns over where it is struck by the
hammer. If it breaks off in small pieces, instead of
turning over, it is high in carbon. If the end frays
out and turns over like a sunflower, it is low in carbon.
The smith thus has something to follow in tempering.

In making tools of any kind it is very important that
steel containing the proper amount of carbon be used.
For example: Steel containing the right percentage
of carbon for lathe tools would be very poor material
for making cold chisels. A good spring cannot be made
from an old file. Steel makers make different grades
of steel to suit different uses, and the blacksmith when
ordering should always state the purpose for which he

wants the steel so that the steel maker or merchant will know what temper will best suit his needs.

DRILLS.

A in Fig. 34 shows an ordinary blacksmith's flat drill. B is a drill with a twisted end. This latter will cut faster and easier than a flat drill but cannot be refined by hammering in the same manner as a flat drill and therefore cannot be made to stand as much abuse as the flat drill.

To make a flat drill, use steel of about the same carbon as for cold chisels. Draw down, round, to a size somewhat smaller than the drill needed, then flatten out the end as at C a trifle larger than necessary so as to allow for filing or grinding down to size. Cut off the corners on the hardy, then allow to cool, and file to shape as shown in the cut.

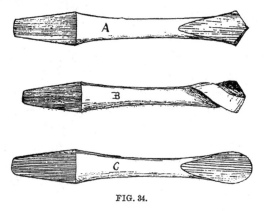

FIG. 34.

The twisted end drill is started in the same manner as the flat drill. After flattening out the end as shown at C, the twist is started in the end by using a small pair of tongs, or by holding the end in the corner of the vise while the drill is turned. After the twist is started the edges are upset by using a light hammer and striking quick, light blows; holding the steel meantime in such position that the hammering will increase the twist.

To temper a drill, if it is a large one, use the same method as in tempering the cold chisel, already described, excepting that it should be made a little harder (purple, instead of blue). In the case of a small drill, heat to a dull red and cool off entirely, then, after polishing, heat up to the proper color by holding against a piece of hot iron or by pinching with a pair of hot tongs.

The average farm blacksmith would better buy twist drills of small sizes, and make the larger ones as he needs them.

PLOW WORK.

The sharpening of plows is a job which the farm blacksmith will be called upon to do very often, and while it is not particularly difficult work, still it calls for a knowledge of steel, and a practical knowledge of how a plowshare should be shaped to run well.

For sharpening an ordinary plow share in case one man has to do the work alone, a round faced hammer weighing about $2\frac{1}{2}$ or 3 pounds is the proper tool to use. With it the edge of the share may be drawn out by hammering on the upper side while the lower side is kept straight by being held flat upon the anvil. For quick work in drawing out a very dull or thick share, especially when a striker is at hand to help, the share is turned bottom up and the edge drawn out by using the cross pein of the sledge.

The greatest care must be used not to burn the edge of the share while heating. He is a very careful blacksmith who never burned the edge of a plow share.

In drawing out the edge of the share near the point, the point itself is very apt to be bent around too far "to land." This condition is not easy to avoid nor to remedy. It will not do to rest the edge against the anvil to drive the joint back, for this would dull the edge. Usually the edge is rested on a hardwood block while the point is being driven back. This accomplishes the purpose without spoiling the edge.

The welding on of new points where old ones have worn too short is a piece of work which is apt to give trouble to the young blacksmith when he tries it for the first time.

A new point for a share should be made of plow steel (a piece cut from an old share is good), and not from a rasp or from any steel high in carbon as such will give too much trouble in welding. The edges should be drawn down thin, and after placing on the point of the share the new piece and the old point should be covered with borax and iron filings. The welding should be done in the fire, at least the first part of it. After starting the weld in this way it may be finished on the anvil; the end cut off to the proper shape, the edge drawn out sharp and the land side squared up. In making a weld of this kind it is necessary to heat very slowly in order that the two parts may reach the welding heat at the same time. Quick heating would cause the thin new point to burn before the larger part got hot enough to weld. No amateur smith should attempt this job until he has had considerable experience in welding steel. If he is at all uncertain of his ability to manage a heat of this kind, he should practice on two small pieces of plow steel before running the risk of burning a plow share.

To harden a plow share which is made of such soft steel that it cannot be tempered in the ordinary way, heat to a uniform light red heat and sprinkle over the entire upper surface powdered red prussiate of potash; this will melt and flow over the surface of the steel, when it should be plunged into cold water or brine. For use in land containing no solid stones it is usually safe to harden the plow share quite hard. This, in case of shares made of good steel, may be done by simply heating to a full red color and plunging into water or brine. It is best to plunge the share in thick side first.

Fig. 37 shows a handy tool for holding the so-called slip-shares. It is a convenience in holding them while sharpening and it prevents their warping. The shares which may be taken off the plow with the landside and brace on are the most convenient to handle in sharpening, and give no trouble by warping out of shape.

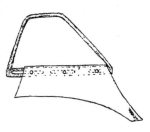

FIG. 37.

SHOEING FARM HORSES.

Because the reader finds this chapter, he must not jump to the conclusion that the author intends to advise all farmers to do their own shoeing. Horse shoeing is not easy work. Neither can the art be learned in a short time, much less from books alone. It has been thought best to tell how shoeing should be done in ordinary cases and to let each reader decide for himself whether or not he shall do the work or hire it done. The instruction will do him no harm in either case, for it often happens that the blacksmith could be benefitted, and through him, the horses which he shoes, by a little timely advice. Workmen in nearly all other lines of work seem to be willing and anxious to carry out the wishes of their employers, but for some unexplainable reason, the horse-shoer does not seem to relish advice, but wants to follow his own ideas of shoeing regardless of what the horse owner thinks should be done.

The late Dr. Dickson presents the situation in the following terse way:

"It is a strange fact, but none the less true, that all the world over the farrier is the one among all our artisans who is least amenable to suggestions from his employers. Other mechanics permit their patrons at least some discretion as to the size, shape and structure of the article desired, but when the ordinary horseowner takes his animal to the shoeing forge he has usually to place himself absolutely in the blacksmith's hands and give him permission to cut and carve at his unholy will, or else take his horse elsewhere, and then probably find himself no better off. The result is that his horse's feet are mercilessly mutilated instead of being left as nearly as possible as nature in her wisdom made them."

There are three or four most irrational practices followed by many country blacksmiths in the shoeing of horses, that cannot be too strongly condemned. First, the cutting away of the frog, which is done by a majority of country smiths, is a most positive injury to the foot and can have no reasonable argument in its favor. The frog is the natural cushion and expander of the hoof and was placed there by an all wise Creator. To cut it out means not only to rob the foot of the cushion which should soften the concussion of every step, but to allow the foot to contract at the heel and become misshapen and crippled.

Another mistaken idea is that the sole of the foot should be thinned till it will yield to the pressure of the thumbs. The sole proper should never be touched by the knife. All loose scale may be trimmed away but the knife should never cut either the sole or the frog. All trimming on the bottom of the foot should be done by the rasp, which will trim the edge and not the sole. The writer has a knife in his shoeing box but he cannot remember when he last used it.

Cutting of the sole or frog in any way works an injury by causing the tissues to shrink and become hard and dry. A frog which has been trimmed by the knife often dries so as to become as detrimental to the foot as a stone or other foreign body. There is never any good excuse for touching the knife to a healthy frog. It will wear away fast enough if let alone. The writer never saw one that was too large.

Hot fitting of shoes to horses' feet should not be allowed by the horse owner. While it may be possible, as claimed by some horse shoers, that a better fit is obtained in this way and that no real harm is done to the foot if properly trimmed after touching with the hot shoe, it is also possible that a good fit may be obtained by cold fitting and the latter process certainly is safer. If the foot be perfectly leveled with the rasp and the shoe be made perfectly level there is no trouble about making it fit. It ought not to be necessary to say that the shoe should be made to conform to the shape of the foot, and not the foot to the shoe, but it does seem, judging from their work, that some smiths need just such hints.

A very common fault among horse shoers is the habit of setting a shoe a little too far back on the foot and then rasping off the toe to meet the front of the shoe. The trimming of the hoof should all be done from the *bottom* of the foot before the shoe is set; and the outside of the hoof should not be touched by the rasp excepting to smooth off any slivers around the edge. The common practice of rasping the entire outer surface of the hoof after setting the shoe, should never be allowed, as it destroys the natural coating of varnish with which every healthy hoof is covered, and allows it to become dry and brittle.

The smallest nails that will serve to hold the shoe in place should be used, and the smallest possible number of them; and they should not be driven high enough to endanger any of the sensitive tissue.

Many farm horses that are not used to any extent on the road would be much better off without shoes for the greater part of the year. If their hoofs are kept properly trimmed the average farm horses will need no shoeing excepting when working on icy roads in winter. By proper trimming of the feet is meant keeping them level so that the feet will not grow one-sided, and keeping the edges slightly rounded off so as to lessen the danger of their splitting or breaking away.

When it becomes necessary to shoe a horse to prevent his hoofs from wearing away too fast, it is often better to use a tip than a full shoe. This will prevent undue wear of the toe, and at the same time will allow the frog to rest on the ground where it properly belongs.

The accompanying illustration shows two views of a style of tip which is in favor among many drivers of road horses. On stony roads or hard pavements, the rubber heeled shoes, or tips with rubber heels, are now being largely used, and promise to take the place of the ordinary shoe. The only serious objection to them is their high price.

On icy roads, or where heavy loads must be hauled, it is necessary that horses should be "sharp shod." For this the ordinary shoe answers the purpose fairly well, but is open to several objections. In the first place

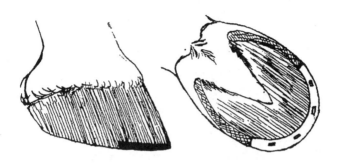

the long calks lift the foot up so that there is no chance for the frog to touch the ground, hence there is no pressure to prevent the foot from contracting; this trouble may be obviated somewhat by the use of a bar shoe, or what is better, a half-bar shoe, which allows of some expansion. The long calks furnish an unnatural leverage which causes severe straining of the tendons. For these two reasons we should make the calks as short as possible and still have them prevent slipping.

When heavy hauling has to be done on frozen gravel roads the calks must be sharpened so often that in case ordinary shoes are used, the horses' feet are badly damaged by the frequent re-setting of the shoes. In such cases the patent removable calks serve a good purpose. The greatest objection to these patent calks, aside from their cost, is the fact that when worn down level with the shoe, as they are apt to be if neglected, it is impossible to remove them without removing the shoe from the foot.

When ordinary winter shoes are used the life of the calks may be lengthened by welding centers of steel in them. This is done by splitting the calk with a sharp chisel and inserting a thin bit of steel, (a piece of mower section is as good as anything), and welding. This center will wear away much slower than the surrounding iron and thus the calk will be kept sharp until worn out. Another way to prevent the calks wearing too fast is to case-harden them with cast iron. To do this heat the sharpened calk nearly to a welding heat and at the same time heat the end of a piece of cast iron till it begins to melt, then rub the melting cast iron over the end of the calk. If it is at the proper heat it will flow over the calk and cover it with a coating of cast iron. Now take from the fire and plunge into cold water. This will harden the coating of cast metal so that no file will touch it. The writer has seen a set of shoes treated in this way used all winter on a snow road without re-sharpening.

A very common mistake of horse owners is to allow the shoes to remain on too long without re-setting. No horse should be compelled to go more than four weeks without having his shoes re-set; and in the case of young horses, whose feet grow much faster than old ones, a shorter time would be better. Corns are almost always the result of leaving the shoe on too long and allowing the heels to grow too long.

To sum the matter up let us follow these rules:

1. Do not have your horses shod at all unless it is absolutely necessary.

2. If shoeing becomes necessary, use as light a shoe fastened with as few and as small nails as possible. If the conditions will allow, use tips instead of shoes.

3. Allow neither frog nor sole to be touched by the knife.

4. Do all the trimming with the rasp from the bottom of the foot.

5. See that the shoe fits the foot; and do not allow it to be touched to the foot while hot.

6. Do not allow shoes to remain on longer than a month without re-setting.

7. When necessary to use calks have them as short as possible so that the frog may touch the ground.

FILES.

In the average farm shop there is usually to be found one, or perhaps two or three files in, generally, a rather advanced stage of wear. With this one, or these two or three files the farmer tries to do all his filing. It he is enough of a mechanic to try to file his own saw, he will have one or two three cornered files. As a rule a corn cob serves as a handle for the farmer's file if any handle is used.

The farm mechanic ought to know that it is more economical of money and time to have at hand an assortment of files suited to different kinds of work, than to attempt to do all kinds of filing with one or two files. This will be better understood after some discussion of the use of files.

Files are classified in three ways; first, according to length, second according to shape of cross section, and third according to cut. The length of a file or rasp is always measured exclusive of the tang, and is given in inches. Files are made in an almost endless variety of shapes of cross section, but those in most common use are *flat* files, (having a width of five times the thickness), *mill* files (with a width of three times the thickness), *triangular* files, sometimes called "3 square," *round* or *rattail* files, and *half rounds*.

The cut of files is designated by the terms, single cut, double cut and rasp cut; and the coarseness or fineness of cut by the terms, *rough, coarse, bastard, second cut, smooth* and *dead smooth*. The *rough* and *dead smooth* files are very seldom used in ordinary practice.

Coarse and *bastard* cut files are used for ordinary rough work where the object of filing is to remove quantities of metal rather than to make a smooth finish. Second cut and smooth files are used for finishing work.

Single cut files are those which have a single course of chisel marks or cuts, (usually at an angle of 45 degrees) from end to end of the file. Double cut files have two courses of chisel cuts crossing each other forming raised angular teeth, instead of ridges. Rasps or rasp cut files differ from the others in having teeth standing out separate from each other, which are made by a diamond-pointed, instead of flat chisel.

THE USE OF FILES.

If the amateur mechanic will bear in mind that the file is a series of sharp, hard chisels he will plainly see that there are good reasons for the following rules for the use of files.

Files should, when not in use, be kept in a wooden rack or hung up on wooden pins. Keeping them in a drawer or on a bench where they are knocked against each other or against other tools injures them and shortens **their term of usefulness. You would not** think of keeping sharp chisels in such a place.

Never use a new file on rough cast iron without first removing the scale with an old, worn file. All castings have a hard scale on the surface caused by the chilling of the metal when it is run into the damp molds. This scale or casing is often very thin and may be easily removed by grinding or by using an old, partly worn file, whereas a new file would be ruined on it by having its thin sharp teeth broken off. When this scale is removed the cast iron is generally easily cut by a sharp file.

Never attempt to file hardened steel with a good file. No toolsmith can temper a cold chisel so that it will cut hardened steel. Remember that your file is a series of sharp, hard cold chisels.

In filing narrow surfaces bear on very lightly because only a few of the teeth can have a bearing on the metal at the same time, and too much force will cause them to cut too deeply and they are apt to be broken off. On wide surfaces many teeth will be cutting at one time and it will be found necessary to bear on quite hard in order to make the file "take hold" or "bite."

As a rule the whole length of the file should be used at each stroke. In order to do this it is necessary that the file be provided with a handle. For this purpose nothing is better than a good wooden handle with a strong ferrule. The easiest way to fit a handle to a file is to have a hole a little too small to fit the tang. Then heat the tang of an old file of the same size as the new one and burn to a fit. The center line of the handle should be exactly parallel with the length of the file.

The teeth of the file are made to cut in but one direction, and the file should be lifted from the work on the back stroke.

The proper height for heavy or medium work to be held for easiest filing is on a level with the workman's elbow. For light work (such as saw filing), it should be much higher.

A file to do good work must be kept clean and free from filings which tend to fill the spaces between the teeth and thus hold the teeth out from the work and prevent the file from "taking hold" of the work freely. The filings from cast iron and brass may usually be brushed out with a stiff bristle brush; but those from wrought iron and steel often stick much tighter and must be removed by the use of a wire brush or card.

Sometimes small particles of steel become packed so firmly that the wire brush will not loosen them, and what is called scorer must be resorted to. A scorer is

made by flattening out the end of a small rod or wire
of soft iron and making a comb out of it by drawing
it across the file lengthwise of the teeth.

TO SPLICE A ROPE.

Every farmer and every farmer's boy ought to be
able to splice a rope, make a rope halter, and tie all
the useful knots known to the sailor.   To splice a rope
is a simple matter, but to teach the art on paper is
quite another thing.   However, I think that by carefully following the directions and studying the cuts
anyone may learn this useful accomplishment.

Figures 74, 75 and 76 illustrate the beginning of
what is known as the short splice.   To make it, first
untwist the two ends to be spliced for about a foot
(more or less according to the size of the rope), and
put them together as shown in Fig. 74.   Begin splicing by placing the strand A around D, as shown in Fig.
75.   Turn the rope toward you and put C around E
in the same manner; then B around F.   Next turn
the rope around; or, in other words, place yourself on
the other side of it and put the end D around strand
A, as in Fig. 76.   Then put F around B in the same
manner; then E around C.   Now pull all the ends
tight and go through the same process again—always
twisting the same strands together so that the spliced

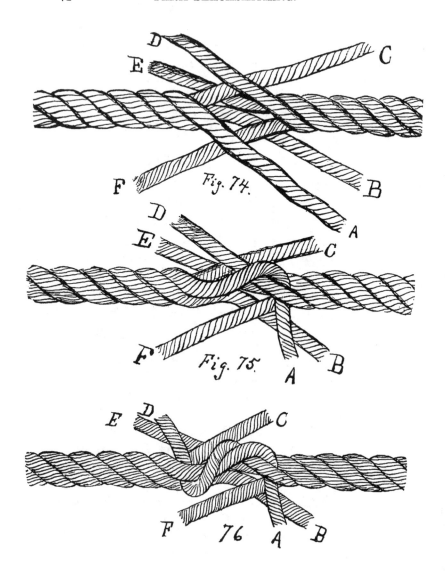

Fig. 74.

Fig. 75.

76

parts of the rope will consist of three strands, the same as any other part. After proceeding for a few inches cut out a few threads from each strand every time it is put around its mate; in this way the splice will be made to gradually taper toward the ends.

In splicing new rope it is often necessary to use some sort of tool to separate the strands. Sailors use what they call a marlin spike (a sort of rude needle), but a short piece of hardwood sharpened at one end answers very well. It is pushed through between the strands and the end of the strand pushed through with it or just behind it. In the cuts the ends of the strands are made short for convenience; they should, of course, be much longer.

ROPE HALTER.

To make a rope halter take 14 feet of half-inch rope, and about 4 feet from one end form a loop by doubling the rope and passing the end under a strand in two places about 2 inches apart (see A Fig. 77). Next

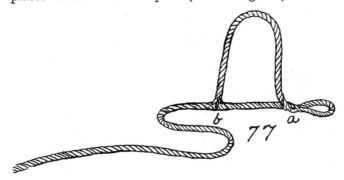

splice the short end into the main part of the rope at
B. Finish the halter by passing the long end through
the loop and tying as in Fig. 78. The end of the rope
should be wound with a piece of binding twine, and
the ends of the twine, instead of being knotted, should
be spliced into the rope so that they will never come
out.

KNOTS

The bowline knot is one which everyone should know
how to tie. It never slips nor comes loose of itself,
and no matter how much strain is put upon it, it never
becomes jammed so that it cannot be easily untied.
For fastening the hay-fork rope to the whiffletrees or
tying a rope around a calf's neck this knot cannot be
excelled. Fig. 79 shows how it is made.

In these days of dehorned cattle it is often necessary to improvise a halter with which to lead an animal. Such a halter may be very easily and quickly made by tying two bowline knots, one to form the loop and the other to take the place of the splice in the halter described above.

The weaver's knot, (shown in Fig. 80), bears a close relationship to the bowline knot, as a careful study of both knots will show. It is used by weavers in tying the ends of warp together. Like the bowline knot, it will never slip; neither will it jam so as to be hard to untie. It is a good knot to use in tying two straps together.

FIG. 80

FIG. 81.

Fig. 81 shows a way of attaching a rope to any smooth or slippery object which is to be pulled endwise; for instance a pump, a pipe of any kind, or a round log. The cut shows so plainly how to attach the rope that a description is hardly needed. A slip knot is made and the rope is wrapped several times around the object. When the end is pulled upon, the rope hugs the object so tightly that slipping is impossible. The stronger the power applied, the tighter will the rope become.

The timber hitch (Fig. 82) is a kind of slip knot used in handling timber, logs, etc. It is very easily made and will not jam.

FIG. 82.

THE LONG SPLICE.

The accompanying cut shows how to make what sailors call the "long splice" in a rope.

The length of a long splice should be about 100 diameters of the rope for large rope and 80 diameters for small rope.

Suppose we have a splice to make in a ¾ inch hay-fork rope. Unravel each rope for a distance of about three feet, and set them together in such a way that each of the unravelled strands shall be between two strands of the opposite rope. Now twist adjacent strands together in pairs as in Fig. 1. This twisting

is done to avoid confusion and tangling and is no part of the splicing proper. In the cut one rope is repre-

sented as black, and the other white to make the operation more plain, and the strands of the black rope are
numbered 1, 2, and 3, and those of the white rope are
lettered A, B and C. After twisting B and 2 and C
and 3 together in pairs, proceed with the splicing by
unlaying strand 1 a turn or two and laying strand A
in its place; continue this process for a distance of
about 2½ feet and leave as in Fig. 2. These figures

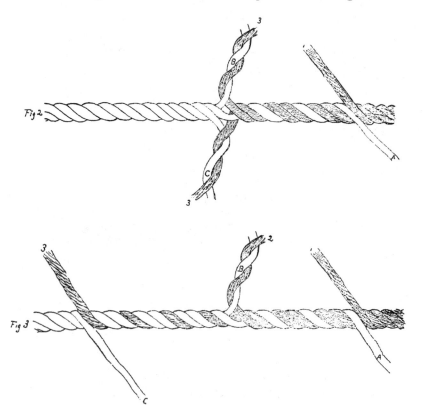

are shortened to save space and the strands are shown
much shorter than they would be in the real rope.
Next unlay C and lay 3 in its place the same distance
as in the case of A and 1. Each pair of strands
is now to be subjected to the following treatment:
For convenience we will take strands 3 and C. Unlay
each of these strands and slip in halves as in Fig. 4;

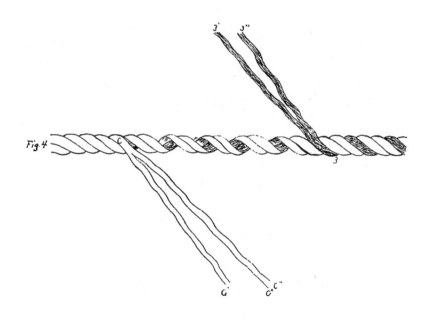

then lay one half of each strand back where the whole
strand came from and tie as in Fig. 5.   Be very careful

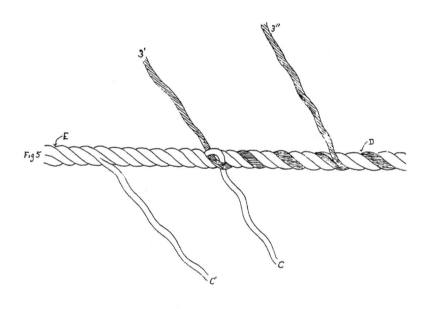

to tie *exactly* as shown in the figure, that is, have C
pass around 3 so that when pulled down tight they
will form a smooth strand and not be lumpy as they
are sure to be if put around each other the wrong way.

Continue to tuck C around 3 till just past the place where strand 3 was split (point D in the cut), then in the same manner tuck 3 around C till the point E is reached. Now cut off the ends of the half strands about a quarter of an inch from the rope. After treating the other two pairs of strands in the same manner, the splice will be complete.

Two or three precautions are necessary to observe in order to make a smooth splice. Be sure that the strands are set together properly at the start so that each strand goes in between two strands from the opposite rope. In replacing one strand with another, be sure to give the same amount of twist as it had in the original rope.

After tying the half strands and beginning to tuck one around the other, pull on both to draw up tight, otherwise a bunchy, loose place will be left.

SAW FILING.

By WILLIAM BOSS.

The saw is one of the woodworker's most useful tools and is used for cutting wood either across or with the grain or fibre. The one used for cutting across the grain is called the cross-cut saw; the one for cutting with the grain, the rip saw.

It is poor economy to buy a cheap saw; and on the other hand, it is sometimes unwise to buy the highest-priced; as some saws are made very hard and are intended to be used only by fine mechanics in dry lumber, and will not stand setting nor rough use.

A good saw for ordinary use is Disston's D 8 with sway back. There are other saws which are probably as good, but the one mentioned is a standard saw and will give good service. The sway back makes it lighter at the point and easier to handle than the straight back.

The size of saws is given by the length of the blade in inches. Twenty-six inches is a good length for a cross-cut saw, and twenty-eight inches for a rip saw. Saws for small work should be shorter.

The coarseness or fineness of a saw is shown by the number of teeth to the inch. A cross-cut saw for ordinary work should have about eight teeth; for rough work or for sawing large timbers seven or six would be better, and for fine work nine or ten.

A rip saw for ordinary work should have about five
and one-half teeth to the inch; for rough work, fewer,
for fine work more. The number of teeth per inch is
usually stamped on the blade of the saw near the handle.

SHARPENING SAWS.

The filing or sharpening of a saw consists of four
operations which should be done in the following order:
First, top-jointing,—which consists in filing off the
points of the teeth until they are all the same length
and making the cutting edge of the saw, taken as a
whole, either straight or crowning—never hollow.

Fig. 1 shows a home-made saw jointer which is used
for holding the file exactly square across the saw:—care
must be taken to have it square or the teeth will be
shorter on one side and the saw will run crooked. A
saw should be top jointed every time it is filed.

FIG. 1.

Second.   *Setting;* which consists in setting or bending the teeth outward, one on one side, the next on the
other and so on till all are set or bent.   The object of
setting is to make the saw cut wider than the thickness
of the blade in order to allow it to run freely through
the timber and not pinch.   The amount of set in a saw
may be readily seen by holding it to the light with the
back toward the eye, when it will appear as in Fig. 2.

FIG. 2.

Care must be taken not to give the saw too much set
or it will run hard and not cut smoothly.   For ordinary
work the teeth should be set out about one-third the
thickness of the blade.   For dry lumber the saw will
require less set, and for green or wet lumber, more.

The teeth should not be set too near the points nor
too close to the blade; about two-thirds of the distance
from the points to the bottom of the teeth is about right.
This we will call the depth of set.   Fig. 3 shows one
type of saw set in which the amount of set is regulated
by the screw A.   Turning the screw in gives the saw
less set; turning it out gives more.   The depth of set
is regulated by the screw B.   Turning it in will set
the teeth nearer the point; turning it out will set it
nearer the blade.   The plate or anvil, C has four faces
which may be turned to suit the size of the teeth.

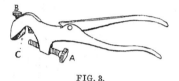

FIG. 3.

Third. *Filing;* which consists in filing the teeth to sharp points. Great care must be taken in filing to bring the teeth to sharp points. If they are not sharp they will not cut and will prevent those that are sharp from cutting. Be careful also not to file them after they are sharp as that will shorten them and then they will not cut. The secret consists in stopping just when each tooth is filed to a point. To get the best results from a saw, the teeth should all be sharp and exactly of the *same length* and shape.

Fourth. Side Jointing; which consists in running a fine file or an oil-stone along the sides of the saw to even the teeth at the sides to prevent scratching. In setting a saw it is impossible to bend all the teeth exactly the same; some will be bent or set out more than others, and if not side-jointed they will scratch, making the cut rough and uneven, and the saw will not cut so fast as it would were the teeth in perfect line. When a saw has too much set some of it may be removed by side jointing.

This order should be followed in sharpening all saws whether cross-cut or rip saws; the top-jointing, setting and side-jointing being the same in all; the only difference being in the filing. In filing any saw where a three cornered file is used, we file one side each of two teeth at once. If you find that one tooth is getting sharp before the other, bear harder against the large or duller tooth, but be careful to keep the pitch or angle of the tooth the same. When starting to file notice carefully the position of your file: *First,* in regard to the angle across the saw as in A Figs. 4 and 5. For a rip saw the file should be about square across; for a cross-cut, an angle of about 45 degrees.

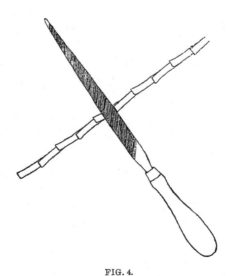

FIG. 4.

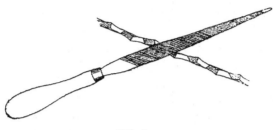

FIG. 5.

Second. Notice the pitch of the tooth as at B Fig. 6. Be very careful as you proceed that the file does not turn in your hand or handle and change the pitch as at A or C in Fig. 6.

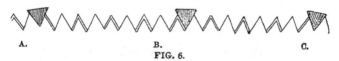

A. B. C.
FIG. 6.

Third. The bevel or level of the file, whether the handle of the file be up or down. Be careful to notice these points in starting and then keep them the same throughout the filing. If these positions change, the teeth will be of different shapes, as at E.

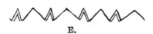

E.

If a tooth be broken out, do not file the broken part, but keep the teeth on each side their original size, and the broken one will "grow" longer each time the saw is filed until it finally becomes of full size or length.

The rip saw, which is used for ripping or splitting timber is usually filed square across; the action of the teeth being similar to that of a row of small chisels, each tooth being a chisel. Fig. 7 shows the shape of the teeth in the rip saw, filed square across. The front side of the teeth should be kept at right angles to the line of the cutting edge of the saw. For ripping hard or cross-grained wood it is well to give the teeth a little bevel by lowering the handle of the file a trifle, also to let the teeth start back slightly, so as not to bite too freely; but for clear pine, straight across, and at right angles to the length of the blade is better. In filing

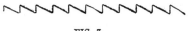

FIG. 7.

the rip saw it is best to file against the cutting edge of the teeth, filing one-half the teeth from each side.

The cross-cut saw is filed in quite a different manner from the rip saw. As it must cut the grain or fiber of the wood in two places, one on each side of the saw, it must also break and carry out the chips or dust between the two cuts.

Let Fig. 8 represent the end view of a saw cutting a piece of timber; *A* being the saw, *B* the timber. *C* shows the point which does the cutting and *D* the part of the tooth which breaks and carries out the chip or sawdust. For cutting soft wood, the point *D* may be longer and sharper than for cutting hard wood, as the saw dust is more easily broken out. In cutting hardwood

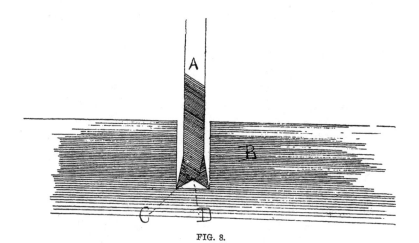

FIG. 8.

the point should be more blunt, in order to break out
the dust as soon as it is cut by the points. The length
or bluntness of these points is regulated by the level of
the file across the saw. Holding the file level will
make the point long, while lowering the handle of the
file will make the point blunt—providing the file be
kept out an angle of 45 degrees to the length of the saw
in each case.

In filing the cross-cut saw it is best to run the file
at an angle of 45 degrees across the saw as this gives
the best results; sharpening the front of the tooth so as
to cut both smooth and fast.

Fig. 5 shows the plan, or the appearance on looking down at the saw and file from the top. The file should be held at about this angle in filing nearly all crosscut saws.

The pitch of the teeth is an important feature. Too much pitch is a common fault. It is well to have a little, but too much pitch will make a saw cut rough and push hard. Fig. 6 *B* shows a saw with no pitch at all, and the bevel the same on each side of the tooth. The file is held level in filing teeth in this shape which is used largely in cutting soft wood—principally in the. buck saw.

Fig. 9 shows a saw with the same amount of bevel on the face of the tooth and none on the back. This form is used in the buck saw for cutting hard wood. To make teeth of this shape, lower the handle of the file, but keep it at the same angle (45 degrees), across the saw.

FIG. 9.

In filing the cross cut saw the file should be held so as to file from the handle towards the point of the saw. Some filers claim that this will cause a rough or wire edge on the face of the tooth. This may be true but such edge will be removed when the saw is side jointed.

No saw, even though the teeth are not set, should ever be filed wholly from one side, as the file turns a slight edge which increases the set. This should be distributed to both sides of the blade by filing half the teeth from each side.

TAP DRILLS.

Table showing the different sizes of drills that should be used when a full thread is to be tapped in a hole. The sizes given are practically correct.

Diam. of Tap.	No. Threads to Inch.			Drill for V Thread.		
1-4	16	18	20	5-32	5-32	11-64
9-32	16	18	20	3-16	13-64	13-64
5-16	16	18		7-32	15-64	
11-32	16	18		1-4	17-64	
3-8	14	16	18	1-4	9-32	9-32
13-32	14	16	18	19-64	21-64	21-64
7-16	14	16		21-64	11-32	
15-32	14	16		23-64	3-8	
1-2	12	13	14	3-8	25-64	25-64
17-32	12	13	14	13-32	27-64	27-64
9-16	12	14		7-16	29-64	
19-32	12	14		15-32	31-64	
5-8	10	11	12	15-32	1-2	1-2
21-32	10	11	12	1-2	17-32	17-32
11-16	11	12		9-16	9-16	
23-32	11	12		19-32	19-32	
3-4	10	11	12	19-32	5-8	5-8
25-32	10	11	12	5-8	21-32	21-32
13-16	10			21-32		
27-32	10			11-16		
7-8	9	10		45-64	23-32	
29-32	9	10		47-64	3-4	
15-16	9			49-64		
31-32	9			51-64		
1	8			13-16		

CIRCUMFERENCES AND AREAS
OF CIRCLES

Diameter.	Circumference.	Area.	Diameter.	Circumference.	Area.
1/32	.0981	.00076	6 1/4	19.63	30.679
1/16	.1963	.00306	1/2	20.42	33.183
1/8	.3926	.01227	3/4	21.20	35.784
3/16	.5890	.02761	7	21.99	38.484
1/4	.7854	.04908	1/4	22.77	41.282
5/16	.9817	.07669	1/2	23.56	44.178
3/8	1.178	.1104	3/4	24.34	47.173
7/16	1.374	.1503	8	25.13	50.265
1/2	1.570	.1963	1/4	25.91	53.456
9/16	1.767	.2485	1/2	26.70	56.745
5/8	1.963	.3067	3/4	27.48	60.132
11/16	2.159	.3712	9	28.27	63.617
3/4	2.356	.4417	1/4	29.05	67.200
13/16	2.552	.5184	1/2	29.84	70.882
7/8	2.748	.6013	3/4	30.63	74.662
15/16	2.945	.6902	10	31.41	78.539
1	3.141	.7854	1/4	32.20	82.516
1/8	3.534	.9940	1/2	32.98	86.590
1/4	3.927	1.227	3/4	33.77	90.762
3/8	4.319	1.484	11	34.55	95.033
1/2	4.712	1.767	1/4	35.34	99.402
5/8	5.105	2.073	1/2	36.12	103.86
3/4	5.497	2.405	3/4	36.91	108.43
7/8	5.890	2.761	12	37.69	113.09
2	6.283	3.141	1/4	38.48	117.85
1/8	6.675	3.546	1/2	39.27	122.71
1/4	7.068	3.976	3/4	40.05	127.67
3/8	7.461	4.430	13	40.84	132.73
1/2	7.854	4.908	1/4	41.62	137.88
5/8	8.246	5.411	1/2	42.41	143.13
3/4	8.639	5.939	3/4	43.19	148.48
7/8	9.032	6.491	14	43.98	153.93
3	9.424	7.068	1/4	44.76	159.48
1/4	10.21	8.295	1/2	45.55	165.13
1/2	10.99	9.621	3/4	46.33	170.87
3/4	11.78	11.044	15	47.12	176.71
4	12.56	12.566	1/4	47.90	182.65
1/4	13.35	14.186	1/2	48.69	188.69
1/2	14.13	15.904	3/4	49.48	194.82
3/4	14.92	17.720	16	50.26	201.06
5	15.70	19.635	1/4	51.05	207.39
1/4	16.49	21.647	1/2	51.83	213.82
1/2	17.27	23.758	3/4	52.62	220.35
3/4	18.06	25.967	17	53.40	226.98
6	18.84	28.274	1/4	54.19	233.70

Circumference=Diameter X 3 1416.   Area=square of Diameter X ,7854.

CIRCUMFERENCES AND AREAS OF CIRCLES—Continued

Diameter.	Circumference.	Area.	Diameter.	Circumference.	Area.
17½	54.97	240.52	38	119.3	1134.1
¾	55.76	247.45	½	120.9	1164.1
18	56.54	254.46	39	122.5	1194.5
¼	57.33	261.58	½	124.0	1225.4
½	58.11	268.80	40	125.6	1256.6
¾	58.90	276.11	½	127.2	1288.2
19	59.69	283.52	41	128.8	1320.2
¼	60.47	291.03	½	130.3	1352.5
½	61.26	298.64	42	131.9	1385.4
¾	62.04	306.35	½	133.5	1418.6
20	62.83	314.16	43	135.0	1452.2
½	64.40	330:06	½	136.0	1486.1
21	65.97	346.36	44	138.2	1520.5
½	67.54	363.05	½	139.8	1555.2
22	69.11	380.13	45	141.3	1590.4
½	70.68	397.60	½	142.9	1625.9
23	72.25	415.47	46	144.5	1661.9
½	73.82	433.73	½	146.0	1698.2
24	75.39	452.39	47	147.6	1734.9
½	76.96	471 43	½	149.2	1772.0
25	78.54	490.87	48	150.7	1809.5
½	80.10	510.70	½	152.3	1847.4
26	81.68	530.93	49	153.9	1885.7
½	83.25	551.54	½	155.5	1924.4
27	84.82	572.55	50	157.0	1963.5
½	86.39	593.95	½	158.6	2002.9
28	87.96	615.75	51	160.2	2042.8
½	89.53	637.94	½	161.7	2083.0
29	91.10	660.52	52	163.3	2123.7
½	92.67	683.49	½	164.9	2164.7
30	94.24	70.686	53	166.5	2206.1
½	95.81	730.61	½	168.0	2248.0
31	97.38	754.76	54	169.6	2290.2
½	98.96	779.31	½	171.2	2332.8
32	100.5	804.24	55	172.7	2375.8
½	102.1	829.57	½	174.3	2419.2
33	103.6	855.30	56	175.9	2463.0
½	105.2	881.41	½	177.5	2507.1
34	106.8	907.92	57	179.0	2551.7
½	108.3	934.82	½	180.6	2596.7
35	109.9	962.11	58	182.2	2642.0
½	111.5	989.80	½	183.7	2687.8
36	113.0	1017.8	59	185.3	2733.9
½	114 6	1046.3	½	186.9	2780.5
37	116.2	1075.2	60	188.4	2827.4
½	117.8	1104.4	½	190.0	2874.7

94

CIRCUMFERENCES AND AREAS OF CIRCLES—
Continued

Diameter.	Circumference.	Area.	Diameter.	Circumference.	Area.
61	191.6	2922.4	81	254.4	5153.0
½	193.2	2970.5	½	256.0	5216.8
62	194.7	3019.0	82	257.6	5281.0
½	196.3	3067.9	½	259.1	5345.6
63	197.9	3117.2	83	260.7	5410.6
½	199.4	3166.9	½	262.3	5476.0
64	201.0	3216.9	84	263.8	5541.7
½	202.6	3267.4	½	265.4	5607.9
65	204.2	3318.3	85	267.0	5674.5
½	205.7	3369.5	½	268.6	5741.4
66	207.3	3421.2	86	270.1	5808.8
½	208.9	3473.2	½	271.7	5876.5
67	210.4	3525.6	87	273.3	5944.6
½	212.0	3578.4	½	274.8	6013.2
68	213.6	3631.6	88	276.4	6082.1
½	215.1	3685.2	½	278.0	6151.4
69	216.7	3739.2	89	279.6	6221.1
½	218.3	3793.6	½	281.1	6291.2
70	219.9	3848.4	90	282.7	6361.7
½	221.4	3903.6	½	284.3	6432.6
71	223.0	3959.2	91	285.8	6503.8
½	224.6	4015.1	½	287.4	6575.5
72	226.1	4071.5	92	289.0	6647.6
½	227.7	4128.2	½	290.5	6720.0
73	229.3	4185.3	93	292.1	6792.9
½	230.9	4242.5	½	293.7	6866.1
74	232.4	4300.8	94	295.3	6936.7
½	234.0	4359.1	½	296.8	7013.8
75	235.6	4417.8	95	298.4	7088.2
½	237.1	4476.9	½	300.0	7163.0
76	238.7	4536.4	96	301.5	7238.2
½	240.3	4596.3	½	303.1	7313.8
77	241.9	4656.6	97	304.7	7389.8
½	243.4	4717.3	½	306.3	7466.2
78	245.0	4778.3	98	307.8	7542.9
½	246.6	4839.8	½	309.4	7620.1
79	248.1	4901.6	99	311.0	7697.7
½	249.7	4963.9	½	312.5	7775.6
80	251.3	5026.5	100	314.1	7853.9
½	252.8	5089.5			

For circles 100 to 1000 Dia . . . . . . Find in the table a circle whose diameter is one-tenth that of the circle specified. The circumference of the larger circle will be ten times that of the smaller one and the area of the larger will be 100 times that of the smaller one. Example:

DIAMETER.	CIRCUFERENCE.	AREA.
50	157	1963.5
500	1570	196350.

WEIGHT TABLE OF ROUND AND SQUARE ROLLED IRON

Per Foot.

Size.	Round.	Square.	Size.	Round.	Square.	Size.	Round.	Square.
1/16	.01	.013	2	10.47	13.52	4	41.88	54.05
1/8	.041	.053	2 1/16	11.15	14.39	4 1/8	45.17	57.58
3/16	.093	.118	2 1/8	11.82	15.26	4 3/16	46.50	59.22
1/4	.167	.211	2 3/16	12.54	16.18	4 1/4	47.95	61.08
5/16	.260	.332	2 1/4	13.25	17.11	4 3/8	50.81	64.70
3/8	.375	.475	2 5/16	14.00	18.09	4 7/16	52.29	66.57
7/16	.511	.652	2 3/8	14.76	19.07	4 1/2	53.76	68.45
1/2	.667	.845	2 7/16	15.57	20.09	4 5/8	56.79	72.30
9/16	.84	1.08	2 1/2	16.37	21.12	4 11/16	58.21	74.28
5/8	1.02	1.32	2 9/16	17.20	22.20	4 3/4	59.90	76.26
11/16	1.25	1.61	2 5/8	18.03	23.29	4 7/8	63.09	80.33
3/4	1.47	1.90	2 11/16	18.91	24.42	4 15/16	64.60	82.40
13/16	1.74	2.25	2 3/4	19.79	25.56	5	66.35	84.48
7/8	2.00	2.59	2 13/16	20.71	26.75	5 3/16	71.40	90.97
15/16	2.30	2.99	2 7/8	21.63	27.94	5 1/4	73.17	93.17
1	2.61	3.38	2 15/16	22.60	29.18	5 7/16	78.50	100.00
1 1/16	2.96	3.85				5 1/2	80.30	102.24
1 1/8	3.31	4.28	3	23.56	30.42	5 11/16	85.95	109.40
1 3/16	3.70	4.78	3 1/16	24.58	31.71	5 3/4	87.78	111.76
1 1/4	4.09	5.28	3 1/8	25.60	33.01	5 15/16	93.60	119.20
1 5/16	4.50	5.84	3 3/16	26.62	34.34			
1 3/8	4.95	6.39	3 1/4	27.65	35.70	6	95.55	121.66
1 7/16	5.41	6.99	3 5/16	28.73	37.10	6 1/4	103.70	132.04
1 1/2	5.89	7.60	3 3/8	29.82	38.50	6 1/2	112.16	142.82
1 9/16	6.40	8.26	3 7/16	30.95	39.95	6 3/4	120.96	154.01
1 5/8	6.91	8.93	3 1/2	32.07	41.41	7	130.05	165.63
1 11/16	7.45	9.63	3 5/8	34.40	44.42	7 1/2	149.33	190.14
1 3/4	8.01	10.35	3 11/16	35.60	45.97	8	169.86	216.34
1 13/16	8.60	11.11	3 3/4	36.81	47.53	8 1/2	191.81	244.22
1 7/8	9.20	11.88	3 7/8	39.31	50.76	9	215.04	273.79
1 15/16	9.83	12.70	3 15/16	40.59	52.42	9 1/2	239.60	305.06
......	......	......	......	......	......	10	265.40	337.90
......	......	......	......	......	......	10 1/2	292.69	372.68
......	......	......	......	......	......	11	321.22	408.96
......	......	......	......	......	......	11 1/2	351.10	447.04
						12.	382.21	486.64

WEIGHT OF FLAT ROLLED IRON PER FOOT

Width.	⅛	3/16	¼	⅜	½	⅝	¾	⅞	1 In
½	.211	.316	.422	.634	.....	.....	.....	.....	.....
¾	.317	.474	.633	.950	1.265	1.584	.....	.....	.....
1	.422	.633	.845	1.267	1.690	2.112	2 534	2.956	.....
1¼	.528	.792	1.056	1.584	2.112	2.640	3.168	3.696	4.224
1⅜	.580	.870	1.161	1.742	2.325	2.904	3.484	4.065	4.646
1½	.633	.949	1.266	1.900	2.535	3.168	3.802	4.435	5.069
1¾	.739	1.109	1.479	2.218	2.957	3.696	4.435	5.178	5.914
2	.845	1.267	1.689	2.534	3.379	4.224	5.069	5.914	6.758
2¼	.950	1.425	1.900	2.851	3.802	4.752	5.703	6.653	7.604
2½	1.056	1.584	2.112	3.168	4.224	5.280	6.336	7.392	8.448
2¾	1.162	1.741	2.320	3.485	4.647	5.808	6.970	8.132	9.294
3	1.267	1.901	2.535	3.802	5.069	6.337	7.604	8.871	10.14
3¼	1.373	2.059	2.746	4.119	5.492	6.865	8.237	9.610	10.98
3½	1.479	2.218	2.957	4.436	5.914	7.393	8.871	10.35	11.83
3¾	1.584	2.376	3.168	4.752	6.336	7.921	9.505	11.09	12.67
4	1.690	2.535	3.380	5.069	6.759	8.445	10.14	11.83	13.52
4½	1.901	2.851	3.802	5.703	7.604	9.507	11.41	13.31	15.21
5	2.112	3.168	4.224	6 386	8.449	10.56	12.67	14 78	16.90
6	2.535	3.801	5.069	7.594	10.23	12.67	15.20	17.74	20.27
7	2.94	4.42	5.90	8.84	11.79	14.74	17.68	20.64	23.58
8	3.36	5.05	6.74	10.10	13.48	16.84	20.20	23.58	26.94
9	3.79	5.68	7.58	11.36	15.16	18.95	22.75	26.52	30.32
10	4.21	6.32	8.42	12.64	16.84	21.05	25.26	29.48	33.68
11	4.64	6 95	9.26	13.90	18.52	23.16	27.78	32.42	37.04
12	5.05	7.58	10.10	15.16	20.20	25.26	30.32	35.36	40.40

Weight Plate Iron, Per Square Foot

Inch	Pounds	Inch	Pounds	Inch	Pounds
3-16	7.55	7-16	17.62	¾	30.21
¼	10.07	½	20.14	⅞	35.25
5-16	12.59	9-16	22.66	1	40.28
⅜	15.11	⅝	25.18		

Weight Sheet Iron, Per Square Foot.

No Gauge	Pounds	No. Gauge	Pounds	No. Gauge	Pounds
5	8.74	11	5.	22	1.25
6	8.12	12	4.38	24	1.
7	7.5	14	3.12	25	.9
8	6.86	16	2.5	26	.8
9	6.24	18	1.86	27	.72
10	5.62	20	1.54		

No. 27 = 1-64 inch   No. 12 = 7-64 inch
No. 21 = 1-32 inch   No. 10 = ⅛ inch
No. 18 = 3-64 inch   No. 8 = 11-64 inch
No. 16 = 1-16 inch   No. 6 = 3-16 inch
No. 14 = 5-64 inch   No. 5 = 7-32 inch
No. 13 = 3-32 inch   No. 4 = ¼ inch

Weight Galvanized Sheet Iron.

No. Gauge	Weight Square Foot	No. Gauge	Weight Square Foot
14	60 oz.	23	19 oz.
16	48 oz	24	17 oz.
17	43 oz.	25	16 oz.
18	38 oz.	26	15 oz.
19	33 oz.	27	14 oz.
20	28 oz.	28	12 oz.
21	24 oz.	29	11 oz.
22	21 oz.	30	10 oz.

TABLE OF DECIMALS.
Equalling Parts of an Inch.

$\frac{1}{64}$	.0156	$\frac{33}{64}$		.5156
$\frac{1}{32}$	.0313	$\frac{17}{32}$		.5313
$\frac{3}{64}$	.0469	$\frac{35}{64}$		.5469
1-16	**.0625**	**9-16**		**.5625**
$\frac{5}{64}$	.0781	$\frac{37}{64}$		.5781
$\frac{3}{32}$	.0938	$\frac{19}{32}$		.5938
$\frac{7}{64}$	.1094	$\frac{39}{64}$		.6094
1-8	**.1250**	**5-8**		**.6250**
$\frac{9}{64}$	.1406	$\frac{41}{64}$		.6406
$\frac{5}{32}$	.1563	$\frac{21}{32}$		.6563
$\frac{11}{64}$	.1719	$\frac{43}{64}$		.6719
3-16	**.1875**	**11-16**		**.6875**
$\frac{13}{64}$	.2031	$\frac{45}{64}$		.7031
$\frac{7}{32}$	.2188	$\frac{23}{32}$		.7188
$\frac{15}{64}$	.2344	$\frac{47}{64}$		.7344
1-4	**.2500**	**3-4**		**.7500**
$\frac{17}{64}$	.2656	$\frac{49}{64}$		.7656
$\frac{9}{32}$	.2813	$\frac{25}{32}$		.7813
$\frac{19}{64}$	.2969	$\frac{51}{64}$		.7969
5-16	**.3125**	**13-16**		**.8125**
$\frac{21}{64}$	.3281	$\frac{53}{64}$		.8281
$\frac{11}{32}$	.3438	$\frac{27}{32}$		.8438
$\frac{23}{64}$	.3594	$\frac{55}{64}$		.8594
3-8	**.3750**	**7-8**		**.8750**
$\frac{25}{64}$	.3906	$\frac{57}{64}$		.8906
$\frac{13}{32}$	.4063	$\frac{29}{32}$		.9063
$\frac{27}{64}$	.4219	$\frac{59}{64}$		.9219
7-16	**.4375**	**15-16**		**.9375**
$\frac{29}{64}$	.4531	$\frac{61}{64}$		.9531
$\frac{15}{32}$	.4688	$\frac{31}{32}$		.9688
$\frac{31}{64}$	.4844	$\frac{63}{64}$		.9844
1-2	**.5000**	**1**		**1.**

WEIGHT IN POUNDS OF VARIOUS METALS

	Per Cubic Foot.	Per Cubic Inch.		Per Cubic Foot.	Per Cubic Inch.
Wrought Iron	480.	.2778	Lead	711.	.4114
Steel	490.	.2836	Silver..........	655.	.3790
Cast Iron	450.	.2607	Gold (Cast)....	1204.	.6968
Copper, Rolled	548.	.3171	Platinum	1342.	.7766
Brass, Rolled.	524.	.3032	Aluminum	159.	.092

To find the solid contents of a body of metal:

SQUARE—Multiply the square of the size (diameter) by the length of the section.
ROUND—Multiply the square of the diameter by .7854, and the product thus obtained by the length of the section.
SPHERE—Multiply the cube of the diameter by .5236.

Publications by Algrove Publishing Limited

The following is a list of titles from our popular *"Classic Reprint Series"*
as well as other publications by Algrove Publishing Limited.

ARCHITECTURE, BUILDING, AND DESIGN

Item #	Title
49L8096	☐ A GLOSSARY OF TERMS USED IN ENGLISH ARCHITECTURE
49L8137	☐ AUDELS CARPENTERS AND BUILDERS GUIDE - VOLS. 1-4
49L8016	☐ BARN PLANS & OUTBUILDINGS
49L8046	☐ BEAUTIFYING THE HOME GROUNDS
49L8112	☐ BUILDING WITH LOGS AND LOG CABIN CONSTRUCTION
49L8092	☐ DETAIL, COTTAGE AND CONSTRUCTIVE ARCHITECTURE
49L8015	☐ FENCES, GATES & BRIDGES
49L8706	☐ FROM LOG TO LOG HOUSE
49L0720	☐ HOMES & INTERIORS OF THE 1920'S
49L8111	☐ LOW-COST WOOD HOMES
49L8030	☐ SHELTERS, SHACKS & SHANTIES
49L8139	☐ THE STAIR BUILDERS GUIDE
49L8050	☐ STRONG'S BOOK OF DESIGNS
49L8064	☐ THE ARCHITECTURE OF COUNTRY HOUSES
49L8023	☐ THE OPEN TIMBER ROOFS OF THE MIDDLE AGES

CLASSIC CATALOGS

Item #	Title
49L8004	☐ BOULTON & PAUL, LTD. 1898 CATALOGUE
49L8098	☐ CATALOG OF MISSION FURNITURE 1913 – COME-PACKT FURNITURE
49L8097	☐ MASSEY-HARRIS CIRCA 1914 CATALOG
49L8089	☐ OVERSHOT WATER WHEELS FOR SMALL STREAMS
49L8079	☐ WILLIAM BULLOCK & CO. – *HARDWARE CATALOG CIRCA 1850*

GARDENING

Item #	Title
49L8082	☐ CANADIAN WILD FLOWERS (C. P. TRAILL)
49L8113	☐ COLLECTING SEEDS OF WILD PLANTS AND SHIPPING LIVE PLANT MATERIAL
49L8029	☐ FARM WEEDS OF CANADA
49L8056	☐ FLORA'S LEXICON
49L8705	☐ REFLECTIONS ON THE FUNGALOIDS
49L8057	☐ THE WILDFLOWERS OF CANADA

HUMOR AND PUZZLES

Item #	Title
49L8074	☐ ARE YOU A GENIUS? WHAT IS YOUR I.Q?
49L8106	☐ CLASSIC COWBOY CARTOONS, VOL. 1
49L8109	☐ CLASSIC COWBOY CARTOONS, VOL. 2
49L8118	☐ CLASSIC COWBOY CARTOONS, VOL. 3
49L8119	☐ CLASSIC COWBOY CARTOONS, VOL. 4
49L8072	☐ CLASSIC PUZZLES AND HOW TO SOLVE THEM
49L8103	☐ GRANDMOTHER'S PUZZLE BOOK 1
49L8142	☐ GRANDMOTHER S PUZZLE BOOK 2
49L8127	☐ JOIN THE DOTS PUZZLE BOOKS
49L8081	☐ MR. PUNCH WITH ROD AND GUN – *THE HUMOUR OF FISHING AND SHOOTING*
49L8073	☐ NAME IT! THE PICTORIAL QUIZ BOOK
49L8126	☐ OUR BOARDING HOUSE WITH MAJOR HOOPLE – *1927*
49L8125	☐ OUT OUR WAY – *SAMPLER 20s, 30s & 40s*
49L8044	☐ SAM LOYD'S PICTURE PUZZLES
49L8084	☐ THE ART OF ARTHUR WATTS
49L8071	☐ THE BULL OF THE WOODS, VOL. 1
49L8080	☐ THE BULL OF THE WOODS, VOL. 2
49L8104	☐ THE BULL OF THE WOODS, VOL. 3
49L8114	☐ THE BULL OF THE WOODS, VOL. 4
49L8115	☐ THE BULL OF THE WOODS, VOL. 5
49L8116	☐ THE BULL OF THE WOODS, VOL. 6
49l8128	☐ THE NIGHT BEFORE CHRISTMAS WITH PUZZLE PICTURES
49L8107	☐ U.S. CAVALRY CARTOONS

NAVAL AND MARINE

Item #	Title
49L8090	☐ BOAT-BUILDING AND BOATING
49L8707	☐ BUILDING THE NORWEGIAN SAILING PRAM (MANUAL AND PLANS)
49L8708	☐ BUILDING THE SEA URCHIN *(MANUAL AND PLANS)*
49L8138	☐ HOW SAILS ARE MADE AND HANDLED
49L8078	☐ MANUAL OF SEAMANSHIP FOR BOYS AND SEAMEN OF THE ROYAL NAVY, 1904
49L8129	☐ OLD SHIP FIGURE-HEADS & STERNS
49L8095	☐ SAILING SHIPS AT A GLANCE
49L8134	☐ SAILING VESSEL SILHOUETTES
49L8099	☐ THE SAILOR'S WORD-BOOK
49L8605	☐ THE SAILOR S POCKET BOOK OF KNOTS
49L8058	☐ THE YANKEE WHALER
49L8025	☐ THE YOUNG SEA OFFICER'S SHEET ANCHOR
49L8061	☐ TRADITIONS OF THE NAVY

REFERENCE

Item #	Title
49L8024	☐ 1800 MECHANICAL MOVEMENTS AND DEVICES
49L8093	☐ 507 MECHANICAL MOVEMENTS
49L8055	☐ 970 MECHANICAL APPLIANCES AND NOVELTIES OF CONSTRUCTION
49L8602	☐ ALL THE KNOTS YOU NEED
49L8083	☐ AMERICAN MECHANICAL DICTIONARY – KNIGHT VOL. I, VOL. II, VOL. III
49L8077	☐ CAMP COOKERY
49L8001	☐ LEE'S PRICELESS RECIPES
49L8135	☐ MUSSON S IMPROVED LUMBER AND LOG POCKET BOOK
49L8018	☐ THE BOY'S BOOK OF MECHANICAL MODELS
49L8019	☐ WINDMILLS AND WIND MOTORS

TRADES

Item #	Title
49L8014	☐ BOOK OF TRADES
49L8086	☐ FARM BLACKSMITHING
49L8031	☐ FARM MECHANICS
49L8141	☐ FARM WORKSHOP GUIDE
49L8087	☐ FORGING
49L8027	☐ HANDY FARM DEVICES AND HOW TO MAKE THEM
49L8002	☐ HOW TO PAINT SIGNS & SHO' CARDS
49L8054	☐ HOW TO USE THE STEEL SQUARE
49L8094	☐ THE YOUNG MILL-WRIGHT AND MILLER'S GUIDE

WOODWORKING AND CRAFTS

Item #	Title
49L8130	☐ 50 POPULAR WOODWORKING PROJECTS
49L8012	☐ BOY CRAFT
49L8110	☐ CHAIN SAW AND CROSSCUT SAW TRAINING COURSE
49L8048	☐ CLAY MODELLING AND PLASTER CASTING
49L8005	☐ COLONIAL FURNITURE
49L8065	☐ COPING SAW WORK
49L8032	☐ DECORATIVE CARVING, PYROGRAPHY AND FLEMISH CARVING
49L8091	☐ FURNITURE DESIGNING AND DRAUGHTING
49L8049	☐ HANDBOOK OF TURNING
49L8020	☐ MISSION FURNITURE, HOW TO MAKE IT
49L8710	☐ QUEEN ANNE FURNITURE - HISTORY, DESIGN & CONSTRUCTION
49L8033	☐ ORNAMENTAL AND DECORATIVE WOOD CARVINGS
49L8003	☐ RUSTIC CARPENTRY
49L8085	☐ SKELETON LEAVES AND PHANTOM FLOWERS
49L8068	☐ SPECIALIZED JOINERY
49L8052	☐ STANLEY COMBINATION PLANES – *THE 45, THE 50 & THE 55*
49L8034	☐ THE ART OF WHITTLING
49L8131	☐ TIN-CAN PROJECTS AND ART-METAL WORK
49L8042	☐ TURNING FOR AMATEURS
49L8067	☐ WOOD HANDBOOK – *WOOD AS AN ENGINEERING MATERIAL*
49L8060	☐ WOODEN PLANES AND HOW TO MAKE THEM
49L8013	☐ YOU CAN MAKE IT
49L8035	☐ YOU CAN MAKE IT FOR CAMP & COTTAGE
49L8036	☐ YOU CAN MAKE IT FOR PROFIT

Algrove Publishing Limited, 36 Mill Street, P.O. Box 1238, Almonte, Ontario, Canada K0A 1A0
Telephone: (613) 256-0350   Fax: (613) 256-0360   Email: sales@algrove.com